Accounting Principles

The Ultimate Guide to Basic Accounting Principles, GAAP, Accrual Accounting, Financial Statements, Double Entry Bookkeeping and More

© **Copyright 2018**

All Rights Reserved. No part of this book may be reproduced in any form without permission in writing from the author. Reviewers may quote brief passages in reviews.

Disclaimer: No part of this publication may be reproduced or transmitted in any form or by any means, mechanical or electronic, including photocopying or recording, or by any information storage and retrieval system, or transmitted by email without permission in writing from the publisher.

While all attempts have been made to verify the information provided in this publication, neither the author nor the publisher assumes any responsibility for errors, omissions or contrary interpretations of the subject matter herein.

This book is for entertainment purposes only. The views expressed are those of the author alone, and should not be taken as expert instruction or commands. The reader is responsible for his or her own actions.

Adherence to all applicable laws and regulations, including international, federal, state and local laws governing professional licensing, business practices, advertising and all other aspects of doing business in the US, Canada, UK or any other jurisdiction is the sole responsibility of the purchaser or reader.

Neither the author nor the publisher assumes any responsibility or liability whatsoever on the behalf of the purchaser or reader of these materials. Any perceived slight of any individual or organization is purely unintentional.

Contents

INTRODUCTION 1

CHAPTER 1 – THE EXPLOSIVE BASICS 3
   GENERALLY ACCEPTED ACCOUNTING PRINCIPLES (GAAP) 4
   FINANCIAL ACCOUNTING STANDARDS BOARD (FASB) 6
   INTERNATIONAL FINANCIAL REPORTING STANDARDS (IFRS) 7
   CHARACTERISTICS OF THE INFORMATION FROM ACCOUNTING 8
   HOW DOES THE GAAP AFFECT THE FINANCIAL STATEMENTS? 9

CHAPTER 2 – ACCOUNTING METHODS 10
   THE ACCOUNTING CYCLE 12

CHAPTER 3 – TWO SIDES OF THE ACCOUNTING COIN 16
   DOUBLE-ENTRY ACCOUNTING 16

CHAPTER 4 – MERCHANDISING AND THEIR INVENTORIES 22
   MERCHANDISING OPERATIONS 22
   INVENTORY 24

CHAPTER 5 – ANALYZE LIKE A PRO 26

CHAPTER 6 – PAYROLL ACCOUNTING 41
   RECORDING THE PAYROLL GENERAL LEDGER 43

CHAPTER 7 – BUDGETING TO MAKE IT BIG 53
   CREATING A SPENDING PLAN: 53
   PREPARING YOUR BUDGET 54
   MANAGING YOUR BUDGET 55
   RESPONSIBILITY ACCOUNTING AND BUDGETARY CONTROL 56
   THE FRAMEWORK AND PROCESS OF RESPONSIBILITY ACCOUNTING 58

CHAPTER 8 – BALANCED SCORECARD 62
   THE BALANCED SCORECARD AND YOU 64

CHAPTER 9 – FRAUD AND INTERNAL CONTROLS 70
   FRAUD PREVENTION 71
   FRAUD DETECTION 73

CONCLUSION 76

PREVIEW OF BOOKKEEPING 78
THE ULTIMATE GUIDE TO BOOKKEEPING FOR SMALL BUSINESS 78

INTRODUCTION **78**

CHAPTER 1 – BOOKKEEPING BASICS **80**

DOUBLE-ENTRY METHOD 80
SOURCE DOCUMENTS 80
END-OF-PERIOD PROCEDURES 81

PREVIEW OF ACCOUNTING **87**

THE ULTIMATE GUIDE TO ACCOUNTING FOR BEGINNERS – LEARN THE BASIC ACCOUNTING PRINCIPLES **87**

INTRODUCTION **87**

CHAPTER 1 - ACCOUNTING IS DIFFERENT FROM BOOKKEEPING **88**

CHAPTER 2 - UNDERSTANDING THE VOCABULARY **91**

CHAPTER 3 – ACCOUNTING REPORTS: THE INCOME STATEMENT
.... **94**

Introduction

Accounting is a major aspect in everything we do. It does not matter if you are balancing your personal finances or if you own your own business, the principles of accounting are something you must know and remember.

Much of what we do today is automated, or done by computers. However, that does not mean you should forget about the accounting principles. What do the accounting principles include? How deep do they go? These are excellent questions.

In this book, we will take an in-depth look at the Generally Accepted Accounting Principles (GAAP). However, I am not going to stop there. What are some things you should consider before we dive into the unknown? Of course, we will start with the basics. It will be when we examine the basics, that we really begin to understand the principles.

Once you start to understand the basics, we will move into different types of accounting methods such as accrual accounting. It is also important to know and understand the heart of accounting. That brings us to the accounting cycle and the familiar accounting equation.

Like in everything we do, there are two sides to every coin. That is even more true in accounting as we discuss the double entry bookkeeping that has swept the world. While on this adventure it feels only right to include a section for analyzing the financial statements.

If you want to succeed in life with your personal and business finances, you must have a budget. A budget brings great responsibility and must be used properly to work and bring you closer to your goals.

With all this information and knowledge, it is also important to safeguard yourself against fraud and outside threats. Take control internally. Granted, with all these principles it is important to bring balance to the force with the balanced scorecard.

Keep in mind; I have given you a small look at what to expect as you join me through this swamp of information. However, just like in the jungles of Africa, there are surprises everywhere. I only gave a glance of what to expect; however, you should look for the additional information that has been added along the way.

You can never have too much information or knowledge; however, it is possible to not have enough. I live by one rule on this highway of life, "Knowledge Is Power."

Come with me and learn the accounting principles.

Chapter 1 – The Explosive Basics

There is much to learn about accounting. Before you can really get down and dirty you must learn the basics. It's like rock climbing. If you have never climbed before, do you go to the first cliff you find and start climbing without any training or gear? Of course not. You need training and conditioning along with a lot of practice. It will take you years before developing the skills to freehand off a cliff. The same goes for accounting. It will require practice of an accounting ninja.

For us to start our ninja training we need to start breaking down the Generally Accepted Accounting Principles, better known as the GAAP. You will find that GAAP has three important sets of rules. The first of these sets are the basic accounting principles and guidelines. The next of these rules are that the GAAP is a detailed set of rules and standards that are set and issued by the Financial Accounting Standards Board (FASB). Finally, the GAAP is the generally accepted industry practices.

If you have a company that has its financial statements public, you must comply with the GAAP standards. At the same time, if your company is publicly traded, the federal law requires that an independent public accountant audits your financial statements. Keep in mind, the company's management and the independent accountant must certify the financial statements and all related notes that have been prepared in accordance with the Generally Accepted Accounting Principles.

Generally Accepted Accounting Principles (GAAP)

As a Financial Specialist in the United States Army you have regulations known as the DoDFMR and the JFTR that governs the finances of the Army. Much like these two super regulations, accounting is governed by the GAAP and the FASB. Using the GAAP, we can count on the consistency in the methods used for preparing the financial statements from year to year.

To help you better understand the Generally Accepted Accounting Principles, we should consider a few factors.

Economic Entity Assumption: It is important to keep the business transactions of your sole proprietorship separate from your personal transactions, and your accountant will ensure this is maintained. There is a big difference between legal and accounting purposes. From a legal aspect, your sole proprietorship and the owner will be considered as one entity, although, on the accounting side they are two separate entities.

Monetary Unit Assumption: The measure of economic activity is in the United States dollar. Which means that only transactions that are expressed in dollar will be recorded. Based on the principle, you can assume that the dollar's purchasing power will not change over time. Therefore, accountants will ignore the effect of inflation on the amounts recorded.

Time Period Assumption: Through this principle we can assume that it is possible to report the complex and ongoing activities of your business in relatively short and distinct time intervals. Keep in mind, the shorter the time interval, the more likely your accountant will need to estimate amounts that are relevant to that period. It is important to state the period in the heading of each of the financial statements.

Cost Principle: Accountants are all about money. From their point of view, cost will refer to the amount spent when an item was originally obtained. That means this amount is shown on the financial statements and referred as a historical cost amount. Based on this principle, the asset amounts are not adjusted upward for inflation. As a rule, they are not adjusted to reflect any type of increase in value.

Full Disclosure Principle: This principle is very important, especially for investors. When you prepare your financial statements and feel that there is essential information that is useful to your investors, you must include that information in the financial statements or in the footnotes. Due to this basic principle, the footnotes of can be huge and attached to the financial statements. Usually, your accounting policies will be on the first note to the financial statements.

Going Concern Principle: With this principle, we assume that your company will continue to exist long enough to carry out the objectives and commitments that will not be liquidated in the foreseen future. If your accountants believe your company will not be able to continue moving forward, they are required to disclose their assessment. With this principle, your company will be able to defer some of your prepaid expenses until future accounting periods.

Matching Principle: Through this principle, you will be required to use the accrual basis of accounting. When you make your calculations, your expenses and revenues must match.

Revenue Recognition Principle: When you use the accrual basis of accounting, your revenues will be recognized as soon as the product is sold or the service has been performed. This is done regardless of when the payment is made, which means your company could earn $20,000 in the first month of operations and still receive $0 in cash payments during that month.

Materiality: This principle provides a possible loophole. Your accountant may be able to violate another principle if the amount is insignificant. This allows for a professional judgment to decide whether the amount is insignificant or immaterial. Keep in mind, the financial statements will usually show amounts rounded to the nearest dollar, thousands or millions, depending on the size of your company.

Conservatism: Whenever the situation may arise when there are two acceptable alternatives for reporting items, this principle will direct your accountant to choose which alternative that will result in less net income or less asset amounts. Accountants are expected to not be biased and stay objective as the conservatism principle will break the tie between the two different ways to of reporting, which means it leads to anticipate or disclose losses. However, it does not allow for the same with gains.

As you can see, the principles of the Generally Accepted Accounting Principles cover a lot and acts as a guide or law for bookkeepers and accountants from all over the United States.

Remember, all these principles are part of the accounting framework. This will include anything from the accounting standard that governs the treatment and reporting of your business transactions.

Financial Accounting Standards Board (FASB)

The Financial Accounting Standards Board (FASB) is an independent, private-sector, not-for-profit organization based in Norwalk, Connecticut. Established in 1973, their primary responsibility is to set the financial accounting and reporting standards for all the public and private companies including not-for-profit organizations. In essence, the FASB governs the Generally Accepted Accounting Principles (GAAP).

The FASB sets the standards for both the public and private sectors of accounting. Look at it this way: the Securities and Exchange

Commission recognizes the FASB as the accounting standard setter for your public company. These standards also stand true for the Boards of Accountancy and the American Institute of CPAs (AICPA).

Through the FASB, we can see the development and issues of financial accounting standards through the transparent and inclusive process that is intended to promote financial reporting. This information is useful to investors and anyone who does financial reporting.

Just like the chain of command in the military, the policies also have a chain of command. There is a boss that oversees the FASB. That boss is the Financial Accounting Foundation (FAF). They are responsible for the oversight, administration, financing and appointing of the FASB and the Governmental Accounting Standards Board (GASB).

There is a combined mission of the FASB, GASB and FAF that will establish and improve financial accounting and the reporting standards and also provide useful information to investors and educate your stakeholders on how to effectively understand and implement the standards.

International Financial Reporting Standards (IFRS)

Much like the FASB, we also can look at the International Financial Reporting Standards (IFRS). In the United States, we rarely hear of the international standards unless you are adventuring out into that realm of business. The IFRS is a not-for-profit, public interest organization that enforces and sets the globally accepted accounting standards. They also promote and facilitate the adoption of the standards. Think of the IFRS as the international version of the GAAP.

Their mission is to bring transparency, accountability and efficiency to the financial markets throughout the world through the development of the IFRS standards.

Characteristics of the Information from Accounting

All of us have high expectations of our accountants. They are professionals, and you expect them to ensure that all the financial statements and bookkeeping is done in accordance with the principles, guides and financial laws that are set forth for your business. There are three skills that you expect from your accountant.

Reliable, Verifiable and Objective: We have already introduced you to the basic principles; however, based on these principles, your accountant should be reliable, verifiable and objective. Let's say you have a piece of land and you ask eight accountants to give you the land's current value. Chances are you will also get eight different answers. Why is that, they all accountants and professionals? The answer is simple! The current value amount is less reliable, less verifiable and less objective than the original cost, which means the original cost will be used. The profession of accounting has been willing to move away from the cost principle due to the reliable, verifiable and objective amounts that are involved.

Consistency: Accountants are expected to be consistent when they apply the accounting principles, procedures and practices, although when there are changes it does need to be clearly disclosed.

Comparability: Anyone who is interested in your company such as investors, lenders and customers expect the financial statements from your company prepared to be compared against another company within the same industry.

How Does the GAAP Affect the Financial Statements?

The basic principles that we have covered will directly affect the way your financial statements are prepared and read. The principles influence three main areas.

Balance Sheet: When you look at the balance sheet, consider it as a snapshot of your company's assets, liabilities and owner's equity during a period. With the cost principle, if you have land, it is shown in the asset account as Land with the amount showing the original price and not the appraised amount. Using the matching principle, you take the required expenses and match them with either the revenues or the time when they are used. You may also have a deferring insurance expense to the balance sheet due to the going concern assumption principle.

Income Statement: With the income statement, we will see a period such as a year, quarter, month or possibly four weeks. When the statement is prepared on the accrual basis of accounting, it will show how profitable a company was during that period. On this statement, you will use the revenue recognition principle and matching principle when reporting revenues.

The Notes to Financial Statements: Another principle is that of full disclosure. This principle states that your company must have full disclosure of the financial statements and the notes that will accompany them. Through these notes, you will have valuable information that will help interested parties make sound investment and credit decisions when they examine the financial statements. These notes are an integral part of the financial statements.

Chapter 2 – Accounting Methods

There are two basic accounting methods that we typically use. You have the cash basis of accounting and the accrual accounting. However, we will be focusing on the accrual accounting method, mainly because it conforms to the principles of the Generally Accepted Accounting Principles. Through this method, we will record your revenues and expenses as they occur instead of when the cash is received.

You will see how the expenses will be matched with the related revenues and reported accordingly. By using the accrual accounting method, the income statement will have a better measurement of profitability of your company during a specific period.

There are two main reasons why the accruals will need to be adjusted.

- ➢ Revenues have been earned but are not recorded in the accounts.
- ➢ Expenses have been incurred but are not recorded in the accounts.

Keep in mind; most businesses use the accrual method. However, not all small businesses are required to use this method. The Internal Revenue Services (IRS) states that a qualifying small business taxpayer will be able to choose either method, although they must stick with that same method throughout the lifespan of the business.

When you make adjusting entries in accrual accounting, they will fall under five main categories.

Accrual Expenses: These expenses are the ones you have accrued but have not paid yet. A good example of this expense is a loan interest payment that will be due once a year. They will typically show in the accounts payable liabilities.

Deferred Expenses: These are expenses you have paid but have not seen the benefits from yet. An example of this will be prepaid insurance. You pay for the insurance for the year in advance. The deferred expenses will appear on the balance sheet as an asset.

Accrued Revenues: These are revenues your company has earned but is still waiting for the cash payment. They will show as account receivables on the asset accounts.

Deferred Revenues: These are revenues that a client has paid you up front, but you have not finished the job yet. They will show on the balance sheet as a liability.

Noncash Transactions: These will represent your expenses and reserves that do not have a cash effect on your business. Two examples of these are depreciation and allowance for doubtful accounts.

One thing to remember is the adjustment you make to your journal entries will depend on the needs of your business. Regardless of when you make your adjustments, they must be done before you generate your financial statements when using the accrual accounting method. However, before you make any major decisions about your business, you will want to ensure these adjustments are made. This will give you a better opportunity to make good choices to move your business forward. If you do not make these adjustments, it is easy to forget about obligations that could hurt your business later.

It is beneficial to understand financial accounting fully. If your bookkeeper does not have this understanding, they may not be recording the adjusting entries. These entries can be challenging and complicated. You likely do not have this understanding. It is a great idea to let your accountant make the adjustments. One thing that will help is to have your accountant set this up in your accounting software to be automatic. That way when you run the reports, they have already been done for you.

The Accounting Cycle

Before we can start to understand the accounting cycle, we need first need to understand the accounting equation. This is the foundation of the double entry accounting. The basic equation is:

- Assets = liabilities + equity

A simple break down is that all assets will be the same as your business equity minus all your business obligations.

When we take the accounting cycle and start to lay it out, there are nine steps. These are the steps that form the endless accounting cycle.

Step 1 – Analyzing and Measure the Transactions: During step 1 you will collect your transactions that are needed for analyzing, measuring and recording. The question is, what needs to be recorded? At minimum you should record:

- All cash sales
- All purchases (no matter how small)
- Anything that's measurable, relevant or reliable
- All events such as the external and internal transactions. Your external transactions are between the entity and its environments, such as exchanges with another company or a change in the cost of goods your business purchases;

whereas, the internal transactions are exchanges that occur within the organization.

In essence, your company will want to record as many transactions as possible that will affect your financial position.

Step 2 – Record Your Transactions in the Journal: A better and more simple term for step 2 is journalizing. Each entry will consist of four parts.

- The accounts and amounts that will be debited.
- The accounts and amounts that will be credited.
- The date of each transaction.
- A simple explanation of the transaction.

Step 3 – Post Information from the Journal to the Ledger: These ledgers are highly important to the financial statements. Each journal entry or transaction will have a ledger that it is posted to. You must have a complete record of all your transactions in the general ledger.

Step 4 – Prepare an Unadjusted Trial Balance: Before any adjustments are made you will create a list of accounts and their balances. This list will have the order in which they appear in the ledger and the totals in the corresponding debit or credit column. The sums of the debits and credits must match or equal the same. This will be your trial balance.

Step 5 – Preparing Adjusting Entries: These entries are journal entries that will be posted at the end of the accounting period after the final balances are calculated in the general ledger accounts, making the required adjusting entries fall in line with the revenue recognition and matching principles.

Step 6 – Prepare Your Adjusted Trial Balance: Now that you have the journalizing and posting of all the adjusting entries, it is good to prepare another trial balance. This is known as the adjusted trial balance. In the adjusted trial balance, you will still show the balances as before; however, this time it will show those totals based on the adjustments you made to the accounts. Now you will start to see the effects of the financial events that happened during the reporting period.

Step 7 – Prepare Your Financial Statements: Using your adjusted trial balance sheet you can prepare your financial statements. All the information is now there on one sheet. Remember, your financial statements are the financial results, conditions and cash flow your investors and lenders will analyze.

Step 8 – Prepare Your Closing Entries: Now that you have the financial statements prepared, it is time to close your temporary accounts and set them to zero. This starts to prepare them for the next accounting period. That means that all those balances in the temporary account will be transferred to a permanent account that will be in the revenues of your company.

Step 9 – Preparing Your Post-Closing Trial Balance: That's right! Another trial balance. This time it will only consist of the assets, liabilities and owners' equity. Basically, these are the real or permanent accounts. This will be evidence that you have properly closed out the temporary accounts. Keep in mind, if you did not close them out, when you prepare the post-closing trial balance there will be an amount in a temporary account. If this happens, you need to go back and close that account before recreating the post-closing trial balance.

After completing the nine steps, you are ready for the next accounting period, and the cycle starts over at step 1. For a quick reference to this cycle, look at the diagram:

Accounting Cycle

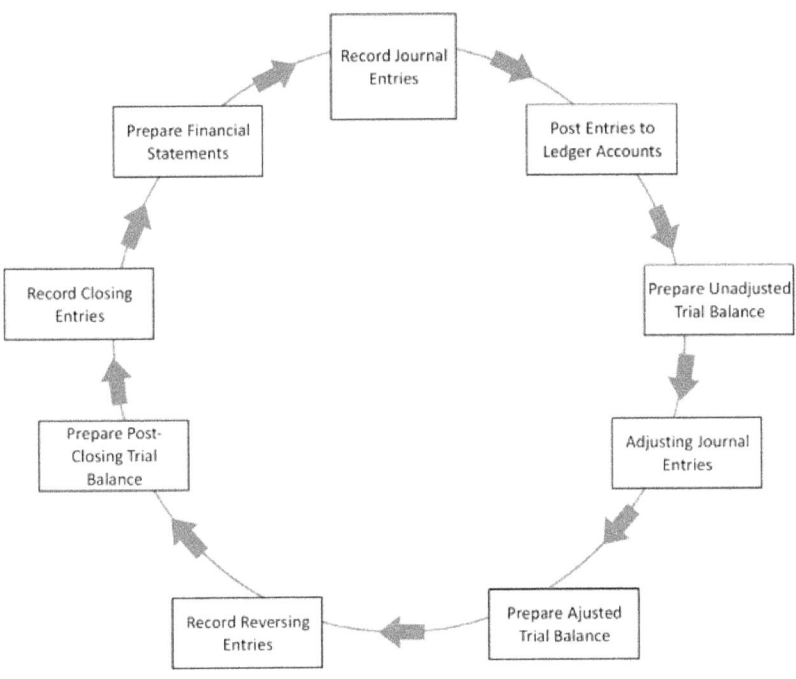

Chapter 3 – Two Sides of The Accounting Coin

There are two side of a coin. The same is true in accounting. When you look at the accounting equations of assets equals liabilities plus the equity, that coin will be the equals sign. On either side of the equals it must match. That means the following is true:

- Assets = Liabilities + Equity
- Liabilities = Assets – Equity
- Equity = Assets – Liabilities

It really does not matter how you look at it. The totals on either side of the equal sign must match. That brings us to double-entry accounting.

Double-Entry Accounting

When we look at physics, everything we do will have an equal or opposite effect. The same goes with accounting. Every transaction we make will have an equal and opposite effect on two or more accounts. To make it a little easier to understand, let's say you make a transaction that will affect liabilities. That means you need to make a transaction that will either decrease or increase the equity to make it still equal the same as the assets or make a transaction in assets that will change the amount to equal the change in liabilities. This is the way to bring balance to the forces of accounting, which means for every transaction, there will be two or more accounts affected. Sometimes there will be more than two accounts affected.

An example of this could be when you are working with credit, and they pay partially and put the rest on credit. These entries will be known as credits and debits. Not all accounts have a normal debit balance and not all accounts will have a normal credit balance. In essence, the credits and debits affect each account differently.

Those who only balance a checkbook may think that a debit means money leaving the account and a credit means money coming into the account. In accounting, that is not true. Debit simply means left side while credit means right side. That means, the debits and credits or left and right sides must match.

This double-entry accounting is an important concept that will drive all your accounting transactions and the reporting of your company. As a business owner, you must understand this concept. This understanding is highly important to manage your accounting process and analyze the financial reporting.

The best example of the double-entry accounting is the balance sheet. This statement shows the accounting equation first hand. You will list all the assets on the left side of the balance sheet. Then you will list the liabilities and equity on the right side. Look at the imaginary line in the middle as the equal sign.

Keep in mind; most of the assets and expenses will have a normal debit amount that increases the accounts; while most of your liabilities and revenue will have a normal credit balance that will increase the accounts.

One thing to remember is that every transaction will consist of a credit, debit and description. They will also have the date and accounts affected. Granted, if you have an accounting software, these transactions can be easier, but they can still be complex at the same time. It is highly important to know the difference between credit and debits and the entire process for recording transactions.

Before we move on, I want you to see what I mean by a simple transaction versus a complex transaction. Let's say you bought some machinery for $5,000 and paid in full in cash. This is as easy as they come. That means, you will debit machinery – inventory for $5,000 and credit cash for $5,000. The transaction will look like this:

Account #	Account Title	Debit	Credit
4050	Machinery - Inventory	$5,000	
1000	Cash		$5,000

Seems easy, right? Now look at how it affects the accounting equation.

➤ ($5,000 - $5,000) – liabilities = Equity

In this equation we are looking at: **assets – liabilities = equity** which is a variation of the same equation as **assets = liabilities + equity**. You can see how both accounts bring balance to the equation as they are both assets. That means, you have one debit that increases assets and one credit that decreases assets.

Ok, now let's take that same machinery and say that it costs about $30,000. You still pay the same $5,000 in cash; however, you need to get a bank loan for the other $25,000. Think about it. How will you record this? Yes, it is more complex, but when you understand the credits and debits and know which accounts are affected it makes it a lot easier.

Account #	Account Title	Debit	Credit
6100	Machinery	$30,000	
1000	Cash		$5,000
7500	Bank Loan - Machine		$25,000

This transaction does get slightly more complex. Now we have both machinery and cash in the assets account. However, the bank loan is in the liability accounts. Here is what it will look like in the same account equation format and you will see how it balances.

- ($30,000 - $5,000) - $25,000 = $0

As you can see, we now have the assets of $25,000 and the liabilities as -$25,000. They cancel each other and give a $0 balance for equity.

Before we really get down to the heart of our accounting ninja training, I want you to look at some of the advantages and disadvantages of the double-entry bookkeeping or accounting. When you think about it, almost everything we do has advantages and disadvantages. It is the same with accounting software, technology in general and the various accounting systems.

Advantages of the Double-Entry Accounting: There are a few advantages to the double-entry accounting.

- Your business will be able to maintain a complete record of every transaction as they are classified into assets, liabilities, expenses, revenue and capital. You will also have them recorded to indicate which accounts are affected.
- The double-entry accounting will allow for you to prepare your financial statements easily as all the records are recorded within the accounts that are involved.
- The trial balance this system creates will help in maintaining the accuracy of all your accounts.
- With the matching principle, your company can accurately assess the profits earned or the losses suffered in detail during a period with the help of your profit and loss reports.
- Your financial position can be ascertained at the end of each accounting period with the balance sheet.
- The beautiful thing about this system is the checks and balances. They will prevent fraud and misappropriation as the assets and liabilities are recorded.

- It will solicit comparative study of results of one year to another and ascertain reasons for change or for making decisions.
- It will also afford complete information with each transaction for the purpose of control permitting accounts to be maintained in all the details as necessary.

Disadvantages of the Double-Entry Accounting: Just like everything, there are disadvantages to this system.

- This system is complex and harder to understand.
- When it comes to the cost of maintenance, it could get high. This is especially true if you have your bookkeeping maintained at different places and need to hire more employees for your bookkeeping department. Keep in mind, the more complex the accounts, the costlier it gets.
- There is a great deal of time required to recording and maintaining this system. This is due to every entry being recorded twice and cross-checked.
- You may come across a case where both sides of a transaction are not recorded. In this case, it is hard to detect that error on the trial balance due to both the credits and debits balancing.

As you can see, there are two sides to every coin. You have advantages and disadvantages of the double-entry accounting system. As you learn how to use this system, those disadvantages do not look so scary. Each account will have a current balance. This is great as it allows for your accountant to produce a trial balance at any time. Keep in mind, the debits and credits will equal on the trial balance. If they do not, there are errors that need to be fixed. No worries though. Your accountant will frequently review the trial balance. If there are any errors, they will be found and corrected before the adjustments are made and financial statements generated.

Looking back at what we now know about the double-entry accounting, the entire process starts and ends with this system. That is why it is so important to learn the ways of the accounting ninja and everything that is offered.

Chapter 4 – Merchandising and Their Inventories

Many businesses offer services, and they do not need to worry about inventory. However, there are a lot who do sell goods. Some of the biggest names, such as Amazon or Walmart, are merchandising businesses.

Merchandising Operations

Merchandising adds some fun to your transactions. Now you are accounting for purchasing, selling, collecting and payment activities. These areas are designed to improve your cash flow.

When you think about it, merchandising operations and inventory really go hand in hand. There is a lot you can offer your customers; however, you need to know how to process each situation. For example, did you offer a discount if paid within so many days? Also, collecting on your credit sales and ensuring your invoices are promptly paid will help with keeping the merchandise operations cycle functioning smoothly.

Your Merchandising Purchase Operations: Just like the accounting cycle, there is a cycle to the merchandising operations that start with purchases. These are the purchases or orders you make from your vendors. When you have merchandise arriving, it is entered into your accounting system for your inventory. You will then sort through items and send back anything that is damaged. If you are missing items, let the vendor know so you can arrange for another delivery or have the amount deducted from your invoice. Keep in mind; if the merchandise is purchased on credit, you will need to enter this into your accounts payable.

Your Merchandise Selling Operations: Every time you make a sale with cash or on credit it will increase your revenue from sales and decrease your inventory. Whenever you receive a cash sale, you must immediately deduct and discount or markdown price from the asking price. These payments are received in cash at the time of the sale, although when you have a credit sale, the customer will take the merchandise home with the understanding of paying for it later; before/on the due date. As each item is sold, you will replace it with new stock and continue the cycle.

Your Payment Collection Operations: When you have a credit customer, they will receive an invoice with all the items purchased during their visit or the accounting cycle. This invoice will have the list of each item, their cost and the total cost that is due. There will also be turns for payment of the invoice. You may want to offer a discount to encourage your customers to pay their invoice early and by a specific date. For example, if your customer pays the invoice within ten days of the date you may offer a 2% discount. Otherwise, it will be due in 30 days. Those terms would generally look like this: 2%/10, n/30. As the payments are made, your customer's accounts payable will decrease while your cash flow will increase. Keep in mind; you should run an account receivable aging report. This will help you better track and collect any overdue amounts from your customers who take their time to pay or do not pay at all.

Your Vendor Payment Operations: Now it is time to pay your vendors. Taking the collections from your cash and credit customers, you can ensure that all your vendors are paid on time. Make sure you are keeping track of your invoices and the due dates. This will help lower your merchandise purchase costs by taking early payment discounts. If you receive items that are damaged or incorrect, make sure you return those items within the time the vendor gives you to ensure you get full credit for the merchandise. Just like you did with your customers, run your accounts receivable aging report to ensure you are not falling behind in your payments to the vendors.

Inventory

As I mentioned earlier, inventory and merchandising work hand in hand. Most of us look at inventory as the items we sell. However, there is more to it. It is essential to know and understand what inventory is so you can fully understand the merchandising operations that we just discussed.

Two explanations will give you an idea of what would be considered as inventory. Keep in mind; the merchandising operation typically pertains to the finished products that are for sale in the inventory.

When you look at the inventory, you have an itemized catalog or a list of your tangible goods or property. They can also be intangible attributes or qualities.

You can also consider inventory as the value of the materials or goods your company holds, which means raw materials, subassemblies and work in progress in support of production is considered inventory. You can also include materials that are in support of activities such as repairs, maintenance and consumables. Finally, anything that supports a sale or your customer service such as merchandise, finished goods and spare parts is inventory.

Most of the time when you look at the categories in your current assets, your inventory will be the largest figure listed. At the end of each accounting period, you must calculate the inventory your business holds to accurately report any profits and losses. Keep in mind, how big your inventory is will determine how often you check your inventory figures.

You should know, it will not be advantageous to your business to have a large inventory. However, on the other side of things, if you have too little inventory, it is also not advantageous to your business. When you have a large inventory, it costs more to store and items can get dated before you make the sale. If you do not have enough inventory you could lose a potential sale. One thing that can help with this is the just-in-time (JIT) inventory system. This system will help you manage your inventory as it creates or receives inventory only when needed and can cut down on costs.

Chapter 5 – Analyze Like A Pro

Anyone who is interested in your company will analyze your financial statements. These can be investors, lenders and customers. As a business owner, you must know how to perform these analyses. Take the time to understand what these organizations are seeing. As you start to analyze your own financial statements, you will not only get to know your business better, but you will also see what others will see about your business. Now I know we are talking about external sources who are interested in the business; however, as the owner, you should be more interested in what your financial statements are telling you. This is the key to rocketing your business into the future and seeing great success.

It is important to have a great understanding of what your financial statements show. This knowledge will help you plan ahead for the future. You will be able to avoid the lows and capitalize on the highs that come from your business. Having a plan will help you stay out of debt and grow your business. It is easier to start your business with as little debt as possible. Understanding your financial statements will show where your weaknesses and strengths lie. Becoming a pro at analyzing will give you that edge you need as a business owner to grow and expand your business.

Through this process of financial statement analysis, you can review and analyze your financial statements so you can make better economic decisions. This will allow you to gain an understanding of your organization's situation financially. As you review the statements, you can identify specific areas during a specific reporting period.

Trends: You will want to create trend lines for the key items in your financial statements over multiple periods. This will allow you to see how your company is performing. Usually, trend lines are for revenues, gross margin, net profit, cash, accounts receivable and debt.

Proportion Analysis: Many ratios are available for discerning the relationship between the size of various accounts in the financial statements. For example: You can calculate your company's quick ratio *(Quick Ratio = (Cash + Marketable Securities + Receivables) / Current Liabilities)* to estimate your ability to pay your immediate liabilities. You could also use the debt to equity ratio *(Debt to Equity Ratio = Total Liabilities / Shareholders' 'Owners' Equity)* to see if you have taken on too much debt. You will use these ratios frequently between the revenues and expenses that are listed on the income statement and the assets, liabilities and equity accounts that are listed on the balance sheet.

As you can see, these analyses are a fantastic and powerful tool for those who have an interest in your business and will look at the financial statements.

Creditors: When you have a company lend money to your company, they will be interested in your ability to pay back debt. They will focus on the various cash flow measures. A creditor does not want to lend money to a business who will struggle to pay off their debt. That is why a financial analysis is so critical. They want to make sure you are established enough to pay them back. A good example of this will be a business loan from your bank.

Investors: Both your current and prospective investors will examine your financial statements to learn about your company's ability to continue issuing dividends, generate cash flow or continue growing at the historical rate which will depend upon their investment philosophies. The bottom line, your investors want to make sure your company will continue to do well enough for them to make money through their investment.

Management: Your controller will prepare an ongoing analysis of the company's financial results. Their focus will be the relation to many operating metrics that are not seen by the outside entities such as the cost per delivery, cost per distribution channel, profit by product, etc. These analyses are highly essential for you to move and grow your company. You must learn what these analyses mean and understand them. This will be a key element to the future of your company.

Regulatory Authorities: If your company is publicly held and files in the United States, your financial statements will be looked at by the Securities and Exchange Commission (SEC). They are checking to verify that your financial statements comply with the various accounting standards and the rules set by the SEC.

Now that you are preparing to analyze your financial statements, it is important to note that there are two key methods. The first method is the use of the horizontal and vertical analysis.

Horizontal Analysis: This is the comparison of your financial information over various reporting periods. The purpose is to see if there are any unusually high or low numbers in comparison to the previous periods. This may trigger a detailed investigation into the reason for such a big difference. Here are two examples of a horizontal analysis using both the income statement and the balance sheet.

Horizontal Analysis of the Income Statement Example:

	2017	2018	Variance
Sales	$ 1,000,000	$ 1,500,000	$ 500,000
Cost of Goods Sold	400,000	600,000	(200,000)
Gross Margin	600,000	900,000	300,000
Salaries and wages	250,000	375,000	(125,000)
Office Rent	50,000	80,000	(30,000)
Supplies	10,000	20,000	(10,000)
Utilities	20,000	30,000	(10,000)
Other Expenses	90,000	110,000	(20,000)
Total	420,000	615,000	(195,000)
Net Profit	$ 180,000	$ 285,000	$ 105,000

Horizontal Analysis of the Balance Sheet

	2017	2018	Variance
Cash	$ 100,000	$ 80,000	$ (20,000)
Accounts Receivable	350,000	525,000	175,000
Inventory	150,000	275,000	125,000
Total Current Assets	600,000	880,000	280,000
Fixed Assets	400,000	800,000	400,000
Total Assets	$1,000,000	$1,680,000	$ 680,000
Accounts Payable	$ 180,000	$ 300,000	$ 120,000
Accrued Liabilities	70,000	120,000	50,000
Total Current Liabilities	250,000	420,000	170,000
Notes Payable	300,000	525,000	225,000
Total Liabilities	550,000	945,000	395,000
Capital Stock	200,000	200,000	-
Retained Earnings	250,000	535,000	285,000
Total Equity	450,000	735,000	285,000
Total Liabilities and Equity	$1,000,000	$1,680,000	$ 680,000

Vertical Analysis: This analysis is a proportional analysis of your statements where each line item will be listed as a percentage of another item. In essence, this will put each item as a percentage of the gross sales on the income statement and a percentage of total assets on the balance sheet. This analysis is usually used for a single period. However, it is useful for a timeline analysis for you to see the relative changes in your accounts over time.

Vertical Analysis of the Income Statement Example

	$ Totals	Percent
Sales	$1,000,000	100%
Cost of Goods Sold	400,000	40%
Gross Margin	600,000	60%
Salaries and Wages	250,000	25%
Office Rent	50,000	5%
Supplies	10,000	1%
Utilities	20,000	2%
Other Expenses	90,000	9%
Total Expenses	420,000	42%
Net Profit	180,000	18%

Vertical Analysis of the Balance Sheet Example

	$ Totals	Percent
Cash	$ 100,000	10%
Accounts Receivable	350,000	35%
Inventory	150,000	15%
Total Current Assets	600,000	60%
Fixed Assets	400,000	40%
Total Assets	$ 1,000,000	100%
Accounts Payable	$ 180,000	18%
Accrued Liabilities	70,000	7%
Total Current Liabilities	250,000	25%
Notes Payable	300,000	30%
Total Liabilities	550,000	55%
Capital Stock	200,000	20%
Retained Earnings	250,000	25%
Total Equity	450,000	45%
Total Liabilities and Equity	$ 1,000,000	100%

The second method for your financial analysis of your statement is the use of the many ratios. There are so many ratios to choose from. The key is to know which ratio will have the answers you are looking for. Each party who is interested in your business will use different types of ratios to give them the information they need. As you calculate a specific ratio for a period, you can use the same ratio for a prior period and compare the results. There are a few basic ratios you will want to keep in mind. Granted this is only a very small amount as compared to how many ratios are out there. If you cannot find the answers with these ratios, there is a ratio that will get you the answer you seek.

Liquidity Ratios: These are the most fundamentally important set of ratios. They will measure your company's ability to remain in business.

- **Cash Coverage Ratio:** This ratio will show the amount of cash available to pay the interest. This ratio is calculated as: *Cash Coverage Ratio = (Earnings Before Interest and Taxes + Non-Cash Expenses) / Interest Expenses*

- **Current Ratio:** This ratio will measure the amount of liquidity available to pay for current liabilities. This ratio is calculated as: *Current Ratio = Current Assets / Current Liabilities*

- **Quick Ratio:** This ratio is the same as the current ratio with one difference. It does not include the inventory. This ratio is calculated as: *Quick Ratio = (Cash + Marketable Securities + Accounts Receivable) / Current Liabilities*

- **Liquidity Index:** This ratio will measure the amount of time that is required to convert assets into cash. This ratio is calculated as: *((Trade Receivables x Days to Liquidate) + (Inventory x Days to Liquidate)) / (Trade Receivables + Inventory)*

Activity Ratios: These ratios are used as a strong indicator of the quality of management since they reveal how well management is utilizing the company resources.

- **Accounts Payable Turnover Ratio:** This ratio will measure the speed in which your company pays suppliers. This ratio is calculated as: *Accounts Payable Turnover = Total Supplier*

Purchases / ((Beginning Accounts Payable + Ending Accounts Payable) / 2)

- **Accounts Receivable Turnover Ratio:** This ratio will measure your company's ability to collect accounts receivable. This ratio is calculated as: *Accounts Receivable Turnover = Net Annual Credit Sales / ((Beginning Accounts Receivable + Ending Accounts Receivable) / 2)*
- **Fixed Assets Turnover Ratio:** This ratio will measure your company's ability to generate sales from a certain base of fixed assets. This ratio is calculated as: *Fixed Assets Turnover = Net Annual Sales / (Gross Fixed Assets – Accumulated Depreciation)*
- **Inventory Turnover Ratio:** This ratio will measure the amount of inventory needed for your company to support a given level of sales. This ratio is calculated as: *Inventory Turnover = Annual Cost of Goods Sold / Inventory*
- **Sales to Working Capital Ratio:** This ratio will show the amount of working capital required for you to support a given amount of sales. This ratio is calculated as: *Sales to Working Capital = Annualized Net Sales / (Accounts Receivable + Inventory – Accounts Payable)*
- **Working Capital Turnover Ratio:** This ratio will measure your company's ability for generating sales from a certain base of working capital. This ratio is calculated as: *Working Capital Turnover = Net Sales / ((Beginning Working Capital + Ending Working Capital) / 2)*

Leverage Ratios: These ratios will reveal the extent of which your company will rely on debt to fund your operations, and the ability to pay back this debt.

- **Debt to Equity Ratio:** This ratio will show the extent that the management will be willing to fund the operations with debt instead of using equity. This ratio is calculated as: *Debt* to Equity = (Long-Term Debt + Short-Term Debt + Leases) / Equity

- **Debt Service Coverage Ratio:** This ratio will reveal your ability to pay your debt obligations. This ratio is calculated as: *Debt Service Coverage = Net Annual Operating Income / Total of Annual Loan Payments*
- **Fixed Charge Coverage:** This ratio will show the ability you must pay for your company's fixed costs. This ratio is calculated as: *Fixed Charge Coverage = ((Earnings Before Interest and Taxes) + Lease Expense) / (Interest Expense + Lease Expense)*

Profitability Ratios: These ratios will measure how well your company performs with generating profits.

- **Breakeven Point:** This ratio will reveal the sales level which your company will break even. This ratio is calculated as: *Breakeven Point = Total fixed expenses / Contribution Margin %*. There is a variation of this formula which is: *Breakeven Point = Total Fixed Expenses / Average Contribution Margin Per Unit*
- **Contribution Margin Ratio:** This ratio will show the profits left after your variable costs are subtracted from sales. This ratio is calculated as: *Contribution Margin = (Sales – Variable Expenses) / Sales*
- **Gross Profit Ratio:** This ratio will show your revenues minus your cost of goods sold as it is a proportion of your sales. This ratio is calculated as: *Gross Profit = (Sales – (Direct Materials + Direct Labor + Overhead)) / Sales*
- **Margin of Safety:** This ratio will calculate the amount your sales must drop before it reaches the break-even point. This ratio is calculated as: *Margin of Safety = (Current Sales Level – Breakeven Point) / Current Sales Level*

- **Net Profit Ratio:** This ratio will calculate the amount of profit your company will have after taxes and all expenses are deducted from the net sales. This ratio is calculated as: *Net Profit = (Net Profit / Net Sales) x 100*
- **Return on Equity:** This ratio will show your profits as a percentage of equity. This ratio is calculated as: *Return on Equity = Net Income / Equity*
- **Return on Net Assets:** This ratio will show your profits as a percentage of your fixed assets and working capital. This ratio is calculated as: *Return on Net Assets = Net Profit / (Fixed Assets + Net Working Capital)*
- **Return on Operating Assets:** This ratio will show your profit as a percentage of your utilized assets. This ratio is calculated as: *Return on Operating Assets = Net Income / Assets Used to Create Revenue*

You have been given the tools to perform a great analysis of the financial statements. Don't get me wrong; these analyses are excellent tools to have under your ninja belt. However, they do have many issues that you should be aware of that could interfere with your interpretation of the results. If you can find a way to overcome these issues, you will become a super ninja, and I will then be the student as you will be the new grand master of analyses.

- **Comparability Between Periods:** Sometimes your company may change the accounts where the financial information is stored. This will give you results indicating a difference from period to period. For example, you may have an item in cost of goods sold during one period and in the next period, it is in administrative expenses.
- **Comparability Between Companies:** An analyst will usually compare the financial ratios of different companies for them to see how they will match up against one another, although you may have different companies aggregate their

financial information differently. The result of these differences makes it hard, if not impossible, to compare your financial statements with theirs. In turn, this could cause a conclusion that the results are incorrect.

> **Operational Information:** Keep in mind, a financial analysis will only review your company's financial information. That means that it does not analyze your operational information. In turn, you cannot see many of the key indicators of your future performance, such as the change in the warranty claims or the size of the order backlog. Remember, financial analysis will only reveal a part of the bigger picture of your business.

I want you to remember the six steps to an effective financial statement analysis. Before you can understand the steps, you should first understand the three key areas that are covered within the steps.

1. The structure of your financial statements.
2. The economic characteristics of the industry in which your firm operates.
3. The strategies your firm pursues to differentiate itself from your competitors.

Start to understand these three areas, and you will gain a deeper understanding of the six steps.

1. Identify your industry economic characteristics.
2. Identify your company strategies.
3. Assess the quality of your firm's financial statements.
4. Analyze your current profitability and risk.
5. Prepare a forecasted financial statement for your company.
6. Value your firm.

Follow these simple steps, and you will be able to analyze like a pro. One analysis you will find highly useful is the Cost-Volume-Profit

Analysis. Through this analysis, you can find out how changes to your cost and volume will affect the operating income and net income of your company. There are a few formulas that are important for you to remember.

The basic equation for the Cost-Volume-Profit Analysis is: *Profits = Sales – Variable Costs – Fixed Costs*

To determine the break-even point for your sales of products: *(Unit Sales x Price) = (Unit Sales x Unit Variable Cost) + Fixed Expenses*

The Cost-Volume-Profit Analysis will help your company determine your contribution margin. This amount is remaining from sales revenue after all your variable expenses have been deducted. There are a few Cost-Volume-Profits that I want included in your financial analysis toolbox.

The formula for the Breakeven Sales Volume is: *Breakeven Sales Volume = Fixed Costs / (Sales Price – Variable Costs)* or *Breakeven Sales Volume = Fixed Costs / Contribution Margin*

The formula for the Target Sales Volume is: *Target Sales Volume = (Fixed Costs + Target Profit) / (Sales Price – Variable Costs)* or *Target Volume = (Fixed Costs + Target Profit) / Contribution Margin*

Now that we have the formulas down, it is time to move on to the standard costs. These costs will be used as a target cost, which is a basis for comparison with the actual costs. They are also developed from historical data analysis or from time and motion studies.

Keep in mind; there is a difference between the standard cost and a budget. A budget will refer to a department or your company's projected revenues, costs or expenses, whereas, the standard costs will usually refer to a projected amount per unit or a product, per unit of an input such as direct materials and factory overhead or per unit of output. We will go more into budgeting in a later chapter.

The formulas for calculating standard costs are:

- *Standard Costs = Direct Labor * Direct Materials * Manufacturing Overhead*
- *Direct Labor = Hours Worked * Hourly Rate*
- *Direct Materials = Amount of Materials * Market Price*
- *Manufacturing Overhead = Fixed Salary + (Machine Hours * Machine Rate)*

When calculating these formulas, you need to remember that all except the fixed salary components of your overhead must be predicted based on the given market conditions for demand and cost of your materials.

Even though we will start going into budgeting in a later chapter, it is important to note that the standard costing system is an excellent tool for planning your budgets, managing and controlling costs and evaluating your cost management performance.

Much like everything, there are advantages and disadvantages to consider. The primary advantages of the standard costing system are that it can be used for product costing, controlling costs and for decision-making purposes. However, some of the disadvantages are how time-consuming it is to implement, the labor intensiveness and expense.

What is the purpose of the standard costing system? That may be a question you are asking yourself right now.

Used for Fixing the Responsibility: If you have an unfavorable variance after variance and it seems not to stop, don't worry. With a variance analysis through the standard costing system, we will fix the issue with the employees. For example, if the standard cost of labor is less and actual cost of labor is more, you have paid more to your employees. That is a huge loss for your business. Who is responsible for paying the salary to your employees?

Management by Exceptions: You can use management by exceptions easily when you use the standard costing. That means you can concentrate on the big projects of your company instead of doing small jobs where they need your supervision.

Study of Time and Speed: When you calculate the standard costs, you need to study time and speed. Keep in mind, as you study, knowledge is gained of new ways to increase your speed in the lowest time. Therefore, the standard costing promotes innovation.

Helpful in Production Policy: Overall, the standard costing has one purpose. That purpose is to help in your production policy.

Helpful in Planning Budgets: Planning a budget may be the easiest part of using the standard costing tool.

Increase in Efficiency: Every employee will become more alert through the technique of using the standard costing system. This is due to the employee knowing that if he does not bring up his performance, he may be demoted. That means the efficiency of your employees will increase.

Easy to Evaluate Stock: Through this technique, evaluating stocks are very easy.

Easy to Delegate Powers: With this technique, it makes it easy for a delegation of powers, mainly because you will promote that employee whose performance will be the best. How will you measure his performance? Simply check his variance.

Chapter 6 – Payroll Accounting

A big part of your accounting ninja training is payroll accounting. Most businesses will have employees. Even if you have a business and you list yourself as an employee to get paid by the business, you must utilize a payroll accounting system. This system includes compensations such as gross wages, salaries, bonuses, commissions and other benefits your employees have earned. There are also withholdings that must be recorded such as federal income taxes, social security taxes, Medicare taxes and if applicable your state taxes. Keep in mind, all these benefits and withholdings must be recorded and reported to the IRS for each employee.

Some businesses may have a payroll bank account. This is great for setting aside your payroll expenses to ensure your employees are paid on time and accurately.

There is a process to have a smooth setup for your payroll. In fact, this is a six-step process.

- Step 1: Have all your employees complete a W-4.
- Step 2: Find or sign up for an Employer Identification Number (EIN).
- Step 3: Choose your payroll schedule.
- Step 4: Calculate and withhold income taxes from your employees.

- Step 5: Pay your payroll taxes.
- Step 6: File your payroll tax forms & employee W-2s.

This seems like a pretty easy process. However, it scares so many business owners. It does not need to be a scary process. It is reasonably simple, and throughout this chapter, I will break it down to the basics so that you will feel more comfortable with payroll and everything it has to offer.

There are some basic payroll accounts you need to remember. These are accounts in journal and ledgers that will be affected.

Cash (Assets) – When the payroll is distributed to your employees, it will come out of the petty cash, which will be used to empty your accrued payroll.

Accrued Payroll (Liabilities) – This account will represent a liability calculated by taking the gross pay and then subtracting all the deductions, such as the amount due to your employees.

Federal Income Taxes Withheld (Liabilities) – Through this account, we will take the deduction from the gross pay or the payroll account. It will be an accumulation of the payroll taxes as a percentage amount which will be due to the United States Government. These rates will vary from business to business.

Federal Insurance Contributions Act (FICA) Taxes Payable (Liabilities) – Through this account, we represent a liability that is due to the United States Government. The money is used to fund institutions such as Medicare and the Social Security Administration.

Insurance Withheld (Liabilities) – This will be a deduction from the gross pay and represents a contribution to the employee's insurance provided by the employer.

Payroll (Expenses) – The account will be the gross pay that is calculated by a payroll accountant. This pay includes salary payments or hourly rate times the number of hours worked.

Many times, a company may outsource their payroll accounting to a firm who specializes in payroll duties. This is mainly due to how much lower the cost could be compared to if you have someone doing it who is on the payroll. Here is a list of the duties that are expected to be performed by your payroll accountant:

- Compute gross pay (hourly or salary).
- Compute the total amount of deductions (FICA, taxes, etc.).
- Compute the total amount due to your employees, such as the gross pay minus the amount of deductions.
- Authorize the amount of payments due to your employees.
- Distribute the payroll after it has been authorized.
- Issue reports to upper management concerning labor-cost data.

Payroll accountants used to required to use two journals to perform their duties. This was the payroll system that was used. These journals consisted of a payroll journal and payroll disbursements journal. The payroll journal was used to accrue for salaries and wages towards your employees to include all government obligations that are withheld from your employee's paycheck, while the payroll disbursements journal was used to pay off these accumulated accruals when they would come due.

That seems like a lot of work. With the great invention of computers and technology such as Peachtree, QuickBooks and Xero, these two journals have been combined into one payroll ledger.

Recording the Payroll General Ledger

Payroll is an all-new type of animal. It seems intimidating. Maybe even a little scary. However, it does not need to be. Keep in mind; every transaction is a simple debit or credit. If you know what accounts are affected and if a debit or credit increase the account, you are golden. Yes, it is really that easy. Let's break it down some before we get into recording the transactions for payroll.

- **Expenses** – These are the amounts already paid.
- **Liabilities** – These are the amounts owed but not yet paid.
- **Assets** – This is the cash paid.

Some of the most common entries you will see in your payroll will be:

- Gross wages and salaries
- FICA tax payable
- Federal income withholding payable
- State income withholding payable
- Payroll payable (wages you owe but haven't paid yet)
- Other deductions and withholdings (i.e. retirement contributions)

Now that you have an idea of the different accounts that will be affected, it is important to know and understand which ones will be increased and which are decreased. Here is a simple chart that will help you understand how the accounts are affected:

ACCOUNT	INCREASED	DECREASED
Assets	Debit	Credit
Expenses	Debit	Credit
Liabilities	Credit	Debit
Equity	Credit	Debit
Revenue	Credit	Debit

I want to take a few minutes to explain why we debit or credit each account. When your business has an expense in payroll, it is increased by a debit. This is due to paying your employee. That means it is an expense to your business. When your employees earn wages, it will increase your liabilities and so you will credit the liabilities. These are your payables. As you pay your employees, the business will lose money, and so it will decrease the assets or be recorded as a credit. We will get more into the different accounts and setting up the chart of accounts for payroll later in this chapter.

There are five steps I would like to share with you that can help you through the payroll process and set you up for success.

Step 1: Set Up Your Company to Hire Employees – Before you can start hiring employees, you need to make a few important decisions and gather all the information you will need for setting up your business. A few of these decisions include the wage and salary types, desired benefits and much more. Along with these decisions, there are a few items you will need to have before hiring your first employee.

- **Get a Federal Employer Identification Number (EIN)** – The Federal government tracks all your tax payments that are made by your business using your EIN. Obtaining it from the IRS is free.

- **Decide on Wage & Salary Types** – One decision you will need to make is the salary level for all of your employees. Part of this decision includes the pay rate and if they are an hourly or annual salary employee.

- **Select Pay Periods** – Another important decision is how often you will pay your employees before you hire them. The most common time frames to choose from are weekly, biweekly, semimonthly and monthly.

- **Decide What Benefits You Will Offer to Employees** – Benefits are a key component of your payroll. This will take a lot of thought. For example, if you offer a 401K retirement plan or a health insurance plan, you must decide how much you will contribute as the employer and what the employee must contribute to participate in the plan.

- **Purchase Workers' Comp Insurance** – Workers' compensation will provide protection for your employees who are injured on the job or may become sick due to the job. Every state mandates it except for Texas.

Step 2: Gather Paperwork You Need to Pay Employees – Now that you have your business set up and are ready to hire employees, you will need to collect the proper paperwork from each employee to pay them. This paperwork is mandatory for setting them up in the payroll system.

- **I-9 Form** – All employers in the United States must verify any person they plan to hire. That is, that person must be a United States citizen or has a right to work in the United States such as a permeant resident (green card). This will be done through filling out the I-9 form and making copies of the required documents that are provided by your employee. These documents may include a Social Security card, VISA, birth certificate or driver's license.

- **W-4 Form** – Your employees will provide information such as their marital status and number of allowances they want for each dependent child. Based on this information, you will calculate how much income taxes that should be taken from each paycheck.

- **Direct Deposit Authorization Form** – If you offer your employees an option for direct deposit, you must get their permission to deposit money into their bank account. Keep in mind; most businesses have stopped issuing paychecks in the form of checks and are now using direct deposit. This allows for your employees to be paid quicker. With this form, you will also need your employee to submit a voided check. This check will be kept on file and is used to verify that the correct bank information is entered into the payroll system. Even though this is much easier and quicker for your employees, it also saves you money. However, if a mistake is made, it is a lot easier to void a check. Keep in mind, if your employee does not want to have direct deposit, you will need to print a paper check for them.

Step 3: Calculate Paychecks – This is where the fun begins. I do not mean to scare you; however, when calculating payroll, there is no room for errors. Most of all, do not manually calculate paychecks. They do get complicated, and you will not want to make a mistake. Think about it, when you pay the IRS, and you have an over or underpayment what are you going to say to them? You cannot say, "Sorry IRS, I overpaid you this period. Can I have some of the money back?" or "I am sorry that I did not pay you enough this period. It was a rough month." Why not make it easier on yourself and invest in a payroll software such as Gusto? Then all you need to do is enter the number of hours worked for each employee, mark any sick or vacation days taken and let Gusto do the work for you with the calculations.

Step 4: Record Payroll – Do not forget, even though you have your paychecks calculated for you, make sure they are recorded in the books. However, before you can start to record them, the chart of accounts will need to be set up for employees and your payroll. Your business chart of accounts should already be set up. Now we need to add these accounts for your payroll. If you use QuickBooks and invest in Gusto for your payroll calculations, it can be beneficial for you to know that they are compatible and that will make things run more smoothly within your payroll system.

The main accounts you will be setting up will either be an expense or liability account. Here is a great list to get you started.

- ➤ **Gross Wages (Expense)** – This will include the amount you pay to your employee every pay period before any of the deductions are made.

- **Health Insurance-Employer Share (Expense)** – This will include the total amount of health insurance that you will pay your insurance provider such as Blue Cross, Kaiser, etc.
- **401K Matching (Expense)** – If you offer a 401K plan to your employees, you will include the amount of contributions you have made to match your employee contributions in this account. This money will be paid to the investment company that is responsible for maintaining the company's 401K, such as Fidelity.
- **Federal Withholding (Liability)** – This account should reflect the total amount of income taxes you have withheld from your employee's paychecks. You will pay these funds to the IRS based on the deadlines set by the IRS.
- **FICA Payable (Liability)** – This will be deducted from your employees' paychecks for Social Security and Medicare taxes and deposited into this account. Based on the deadlines, these funds will be paid to the IRS.
- **FUTA Payable (Liability)** – Under the Federal Unemployment Tax Act (FUTA), you must pay a tax rate of 6% on the first $7,000 that your employee earns. You will need to fill out a form 940 and file it annually to report the payments made for the unemployment taxes. Even though the form is only filed annually, you may be required to submit the payments more often than that.
- **SUTA Payable (Liability)** – This account should include the state unemployment taxes that you are responsible for paying.
- **State Disability (Liability)** – This account will include the state disability taxes that has been withheld from your employees. Note that this is only if your state requires these taxes.

- **Workers Compensation (Liability)** – In this account, you need to reflect the amount of workers compensation due.

- **Employee Health Insurance Payable (Liability)** – This account includes the amount that is withheld from your employee's paychecks for their health insurance coverage. It will reduce the amount of health insurance paid by you as the employer.

- **401K Employee Contribution (Liability)** – All your employee 401K contributions that are withheld from their paycheck will be recorded in this account. This money will be paid to the investment company that is responsible for the 401K such as Fidelity.

- **Accrued Vacation Payable (Liability)** – If you offer your employees paid time off, then you will need to keep track of the amount of time they have earned on the books. When your employee earns a certain number of vacation hours each pay period, it will be recorded in this account as accrued vacation, which means it is money you owe to your employee. Therefore, if your employee is fired or quits, you will include this money in their final paycheck.

- **Accrued Sick Payable (Liability)** – Much like the accrued vacation pay, you will need to keep track of the amount of sick pay your employee has earned on the books. You will be able to establish how much sick pay an employee would earn per pay period.

Step 5: File & Pay Payroll Taxes – Whenever you start a business, there are already a lot of forms you need to work with. Once you start hiring employees, there is a lot to be added. As the requirements are different for each state, I am going to focus on what the federal government requires. However, I will put in some general information for the state and local taxes, but you will need to consult your state tax commission for the most accurate information.

Any time you have employees, there will be four main forms you will be required to be completed for you to report your payroll tax information.

- **IRS Form 941** – This form is the Employer's QUARTERLY Federal Tax Return. It will need to be filed after the quarter has ended and within the first month of the new quarter such as 30 April, 31 July, 31 October and 31 January.

    When you file the form 941, you will use the form to report the total Social Security and Medicare taxes (FICA) that has been withheld from all your employee's paychecks. This will include the employer share of the same taxes. Even though this form is filed quarterly, you will want to check and verify to make sure you do not need to file on a monthly or semimonthly basis.

- **IRS Form 940** – This form is the Employer's Annual Federal Unemployment (FUTA) Tax Return. This return is filed after the tax you're during that first month by 31 January.

    Based on the Federal Unemployment Tax Act (FUTA), as an employer, you must pay a tax rate of 6% on the first $7,000 earned by each employee. Even though this form must be filed annually to report your payments made for the unemployment tax, you may be required to submit your payments more often based on the amount that is due.

- **IRS Form W**-2 – This form is the Wages and Tax Statement that is prepared for each employee. This form must be electronically submitted to the Social Security Administration (SSA) office. This must be done prior to 31 January in the year following the preceding tax year. At the same time, the form must also be mailed or made available at the business by 31 January.

- ➢ **IRS Form W**-3 – This form is the Transmittal of Wage and Tax Statements. This form must be electronically submitted to the Social Security Administration (SSA) office. This must be done prior to 31 January in the year following the preceding tax year. This is basically a summary of all your W-2's issued to your employees. It will be filed at the same time as your W-2s.

Even though each state may have differences with the taxes on that level, there is some basic information I can give you pertaining to them.

- ➢ **State Income Taxes** – Not all states have a state income tax; however, those states who do will require you to withhold this tax from your employee's paycheck. If you take in a salary from the business as the owner, it will need to be paid from your salary as well. The states that do not have state income taxes are: Alaska, Florida, New Hampshire, Nevada, South Dakota, Tennessee, Texas, Washington and Wyoming.

- ➢ **State Unemployment Taxes (SUTA)** – This tax is usually required by the states and the typical rate is around 2% to 5%. This will vary from state to state and your turnover for employees. If you lay-off or fire employees, this rate could be on the higher end. The state should be informing you each year of the new rates.

- ➢ **Workers Compensation** – Even though this is not a tax, it is still required by most states for you to have upon hiring your first employee. The rates do vary depending on your industry.

- ➢ **Sales and Use Tax** – Anyone who sells a product or service will usually need to pay sales tax to your local or state agency. Granted if you sell to customers who are out-of-state, you may be liable for a use tax instead of a sales tax.

- **Excise Tax** – Sometimes you may sell items that are deemed harmful to the public. Then you will have an excise tax, which is also known as the sin tax. That means items such as alcohol and tobacco will have this tax. However, there are items such as tires, fishing pole and vehicle trailers that also have this tax. The tax is generally collected by the federal government, although there are some states, counties and local agencies who also collect this tax. Make sure you check with your local tax agency for more information on this.
- **Business Registration** – Your business will need to obtain a business license. This will be done through your local office where most states will charge a fee if you chose to incorporate.

Chapter 7 – Budgeting to Make It Big

One of the most significant aspects that need to be included in your planning will be your budget. It does not matter if you are a small freelancing business with no employees or a big corporation with thousands of employees. The point is, if you are going to have a business, no matter how big or small it may be; the budget is a key aspect.

Besides the question of how you are going to finance your business, the question also arises of how you are going to spend the money to help your business grow. That is where budgeting comes into play. The great thing about creating a budget is how it allows for you to predetermine if you will have enough financing for your business and all the expenses.

There are a few different areas we need to cover. Knowing how you are spending the money is only part of the battle. You also need to know how to create the budget and manage the budget once it has been created.

Creating a Spending Plan:

Creating a spending plan is an essential part of creating your budget. The information you gather for the spending plan will be used for forming the budget. This process comes with four steps you must follow.

Step 1 – Identify Income: Take the time to identify all your income that will be or is coming into the business.

Step 2 – List Expenses: Take the time to review your expenses your business may have. While you are at it, create an expense tracker for easy access to all your expenses.

Step 3 – Compare Your Income and Expenses: Look at your income and expenses and see how much income you got to work with and the expenses that must be paid with that income.

Step 4 – Set Priorities and Make Changes: As you go through your income and expenses, set your priorities. Each business will have different priorities based on the type of goods or services they offer. Therefore, make sure these are customized to fit your business.

Preparing Your Budget

Many businesses think they can search for a template for a budget and just fill in the information. This is a good start when looking for a good format. However, that is not catered to your business. There are an additional four steps for you to follow that will help you prepare your budget.

Step 1 – Identify Your Goals: You must have some type of goals for your business. Start by identifying them as you prepare for your budget. I like making a space for the goals on the budget sheet directly. This way it is a constant reminder of what my goals are.

Step 2 – Review What You Have: Take the time to review all the information you have collected and revise it if needed. This is a process that takes a step back for one last review of the spending plan.

Step 3 – Define Your Costs: As you go through each expense you must start to determine the cost of each line that will be on your budget.

Step 4 – Create Your Budget: Finally, it is time to create your budget. You can do this by hand or on the computer. I like using Excel as it makes it easy to format and review each budget from month to month. This is where you will start to put those costs in writing. If you do this by hand, make sure to use a pencil in case you need to change anything on the budget.

Managing Your Budget

Once you have created your budget and are ready to rock n roll, now you need to manage this report. One thing to keep in mind when you are managing your budget is how the previous steps are like an endless circle. You will find that you are continuously revising and working on your budget as your business is active.

Step 1 – Set Goals: These goals should be set from the beginning. Have a place for them to be listed right on your budget sheet. However, your goals will not stay the same throughout the lifespan of your business. As the business grows, so will your goals. Always review your goals each month as you prepare the next budget and ask yourself, "Are my goals still the same or is there something I need to change?"

Step 2 – Calculate Your Income and Expenses: Every month you need to calculate your income and expenses. They may not be the same from month to month. Maybe you took on a new expense or started getting more sales.

Step 3 – Analyze Your Spending and Balance Your Checkbook: Take the time to analyze and see where you are spending the business income. Make sure you are balancing your checkbook and reconciling it with your records.

Step 4 – Revisit Your Original Budget: Always look at the original budget or the previous budgets that have been prepared. Perhaps you have already revised the original budget, look at the last revision and compare it with all the budgets that have been prepared and the original budget. Ask yourself, "How are they different?" If you notice more income during one month after the expenses have been deducted then ask, "What did I do differently at that time?"

Step 5 – Commitment: One of the key elements is your commitment to the budget you created. I have seen too many companies fail because they do not commit to follow their budget.

Step 6 – Wants vs Needs: So many times there are things we want for our business, but we do not need them. On the other hand, there are things we need for the company to help us grow and expand. A great philosophy in handling this is, "Think about it seven times and ask yourself; do you need it for the growth of your company or do you want it?" Maybe later as your company is growing, you may be able to start adding some of your wants into the budget. However, do this gradually and as you can afford it as the company grows.

Step 7 – Seasonal Expenses: Think about what your business does. Do you have seasonal expenses? You will need to add this to your budget during those months the extra expenses occur.

It is essential that you fully understand the process of budget planning and the preparation system. Once you have created your first budget, the rest will become easier to manage and create through revisions.

Responsibility Accounting and Budgetary Control

You have probably noticed that I combined responsibility accounting and budgetary control. This is mainly because they tend to work together. These two areas intertwine in relationship with each other. Keep this in mind; the manager will be responsible for only that part or area they can control. That means, if you are the manager and you do not control that area then you are not responsible for that specific area. The manager in control will be the one who is accountable. Most functions within your business will be controllable.

We talked about the standard costing earlier. Through the costing method, we get help with the ascertainment of the differences that will work in the business and the planning performance which will help in making the comparisons.

Often you will see responsibility accounting misinterpreted as budgetary control or vice versa. However, they are different. For example:

- ➢ Budgetary control does not differentiate between the controllable and non-controllable costs; whereas responsibility accounting does distinguish between the controllable and non-controllable cost – taking into consideration only the controllable costs.
- ➢ Budgetary control does not emphasize the performance appraisal reports. However, the responsibility accounting does stress the performance appraisal and will export the report from all the manager centers.

With that said, there are two types of budgets you may be working with. It is important to understand each.

Flexible Budget: Through this type of budget, we are flexible with the firm's level of operations. In fact, it is designed for just that which means that as the situation changes, so does the budget. It is considered dynamic in nature and works for the requirements of your firm.

Fixed Budget: With this type of budget, as the level of your firm's operations change, the budget will stay the same. It does not matter what your business does; you will not see any changes in a fixed budget. In other words, your business is not dynamic in nature.

When you have a big business, it is not easy to handle everything by yourself. This is where budgetary control and responsibility accounting start to work together. The budgetary control is a huge job. Therefore, we need to take that control and start to delegate the responsibilities down to smaller departments. By doing this, each department will be responsible for their own section and will help the maintenance of efficiency of your business. Each of these small departments or centers are known as the responsibility centers. They will look after the work for their own department and report to the main control center accordingly. It is much like the chain of command in the military where you have a team leader who is over six soldiers. That team leader will report to a squad leader. The squad leader will report to the detachment sergeant. The detachment sergeant will report to the first sergeant, and the first sergeant will report to the sergeant major. Through using this technique, you will find a better and more efficient way to control your business. There usually are four different types of responsibility centers.

Cost Center: Through the cost center, the only concern they have is the cost, such as taking care that the cost must be kept in check and at the same time to minimize the cost as much as they can.

Revenue Center: Through this center, they will deal with the pricing of the product in such a manner that the costs of the business are covered, and the desired profit will be met. This department will be concerned with the sale of the products.

Investment Center: With this center, the output will be comparable with the return on investments to achieve the maximum returns.

Profit Center: This center cares about the earning of profit. In essence, the revenue minus the expenses will get us the profit. This department aims to maximize the profits of your business.

The Framework and Process of Responsibility Accounting

Now that we have an idea of what responsibility accounting and budgeting control are, it is time to start to understand the framework and how they work together.

- ➢ The organization must be divided into the proper departments.

- Every department must be well organized.
- Each department must have a manager and is required to know what their job duties are.
- The performance report must be presented in a defined format which will be only reported on the activities that are controllable.

Keep in mind, the process of the responsibility accounting is mainly concerned with communication. It does not matter if you are in the military, a small business, a large business or a corporation; communication is key, and it must be effective for your organization to succeed. There are four main steps you should follow:

- You must choose your managers very carefully for each responsibility center. They should be someone who you see as a leader and who will ensure things get done to your high standards.
- As each manager is assigned, they must be informed as to what their job is and their functions within that role.
- From time to time there must be a performance report filed with complete details.
- The suggestion should be given for the improvement of performance as well as corrective measures that should be taken to get proper results.

Much like everything, there are advantages and disadvantages. A few of the advantages are a vital part of the association and are:

- The responsibility accounting will help in better understanding the functions of your business and the process of budgeting. It will show the importance of budgets as they are set to your business. It also helps in the planning. If you do not have a plan, your business operations will fail. When you think about it, if you have a failing plan, then you planned to fail.

- The responsibility accounting will help in the quantitative presentation of the data. This presentation will give a basis for the comparison of the data and will help through the ascertaining the shortfalls.
- The responsible accounting will fix the responsibility of the center which will help measure the financial performance of your responsibility center.
- The responsibility accounting will help in controlling the price expenses of the individuals. That means it helps in the managing of expenses as well as the cost reduction.

As I mentioned, with all advantages there are some disadvantage or limitations.

- The departments of your business are intertwined where sometimes it is not possible to fix the responsibilities of the departments. That means the inter-department makes it difficult for the business to ascertain the responsibilities to be assigned to a specific department.
- The responsible accounting will require a well-developed and well figured out system of communication and reporting. There will be a need for an efficient reporting system which will be easily understood and is reliable.
- The focus of the responsible accounting are the goals of your business. This could lead to contradictions between the interests of the individual and your organization's interests which could lead to some serious consequences.
- The system will completely ignore the qualitative aspects and will give importance to the quantitative aspects and results instead. This is the reason the accounting system is rendered inefficient.
- The aim may face some resistance from your employees while at the same time ignoring the interests of the individuals within the formation of your policies. This also

means it will continue to ignore the personal reactions of the personnel involved in the implementation of the system.

In short, when used properly you will see great success within your business. Budgets are a key element to see this success.

Chapter 8 – Balanced Scorecard

A balanced scorecard will be used within both the public and private sectors,. What is a balanced scorecard? It can be used to track progress over time of some entities, such as an enterprise, employee or a business unit and shows in a graphical representation the specific goal or goals they are working towards.

The best way to look at the scorecard is as a strategy performance management tool. It is a design method and automation tool with a semi-standard structured report. Through this tool, you and your managers can keep track of the execution of activities by the staff that are within your control and to monitor the consequences that will arise from these actions.

The balanced scorecard can be used in the various departments. For example, it will demonstrate the strategic value of HR by defining and measuring its contribution in concrete and understandable terms. It will leverage the strategic non-financial performance measurements alongside the traditional financial metrics.

The balanced scorecard has four perspectives that you must know and understand.

The Financial Perspective: With this perspective, we focus on the financial performance of your organization. It will typically cover the revenue and profit targets of the commercial companies along with the budget and cost-saving targets of not-for-profit organizations. Your financial health of the organization is a critical perspective for your managers to track. It is also important for you to note that the financial performance is usually the result of a good performance in the other three perspectives.

The Customer Perspective: This perspective will focus on the performance targets as they will relate to your customers and the market. Usually, it will cover the growth and service targets of your customers to include the market share and branding objectives. The typical measures and KPIs in this perspective will consist of your customer's satisfaction, service levels, net promoter score, market share and brand awareness.

The Internal Process Perspective: This perspective will focus on the internal operational goals and will cover the objectives as they relate to the key processes necessary to deliver your customer objectives. Your business will outline the internal business process goals and the things your organization must do well internally for you to push performance. The typical measures and KPIs will include the process improvements, quality optimization, and the capacity utilization.

The Learning and Growth Perspective: This perspective will focus on the intangible drivers of your future and is often broken down into three components. The first component is the human capital, such as skills, talent, and knowledge. The second component will be the information capital such as the databases, information systems, networks and technology infrastructure. Finally, the third component will be the organization capital, such as the culture, leadership, employee alignment, teamwork and knowledge management. The typical measures and KPIs will include your staff engagement, skills assessments, performance management scores and your corporate culture audits.

These are only the basic perspectives of your scorecard. They clearly have a broad range where some companies and businesses have extended these four perspectives and added other perspectives for them to highlight areas of performance such as health and safety or corporate social responsibility and environmental performances.

Each company is different; however, the four basic perspectives will always stay the same. You can add to these perspectives, but you cannot take them away.

The Balanced Scorecard and You

Keep in mind; the balanced scorecard is a strategic performance measurement model or tool. It was developed by Robert Kaplan and David Norton with the objective to translate your organization's mission and vision into actual or operational actions. In essence, it helps with the strategic planning. With this great tool, you will be provided information on the chosen strategy, managing feedback, and the learning process and be able to determine the target figures. You will notice the operational actions are set up with a measurable indicator that will provide support for understanding and adjusting the chosen strategy.

The starting point for your balanced scorecard will be through the vision and the strategy that are viewed through the four perspectives. Let's take some time to further go into detail about these perspectives.

The Financial Perspective: This perspective is essential for all your shareholders and institutions that provide financial backing for your business. You can consider that as a quantitative benchmark that is based on figures from the past. It will also offer some reliable insight into the operational management and the sustainability of the chosen strategy. This will give added value to the other perspectives and be translated into financial success.

Financial	Objectives	Measures	Targets	Initiatives
"To succeed financially how should we appear to our shareholders?"				

Customer Perspective: Each organization will serve a specific need in the market. This is done through your customers who are the target group you will have in mind. Customers will determine the quality, price, service and the acceptable margins of the products or services. Your business should always try to meet the expectations of your customers. These expectations are ever changing and could change at any time. Keep in mind, some competitors have a considerable influence on the expectations of your customers. Therefore, you should ask yourself, "How attractive should we appear to our customers?"

Customer	Objectives	Measures	Targets	Initiatives
"To achieve our vision, how should we appear to our customers?"				

Internal Business Processes: Through this perspective, the question should be, "What internal processes have actually added value to your organization and what activities need to be carried out within these processes?" With added value, you will see the expressed performance that is geared towards the customer which will result from the optimal alignment between processes, activities and the decisions. That means you are faced with the question through this perspective, "What must we excel at to satisfy our customers and shareholders to include our financial brokers?"

Internal Business Processes "To satisify our shareholders and customers, what business processes must we excel at?"	Objectives	Measures	Targets	Initiatives

Learn and Growth: Your organization's learning ability and innovation indicates whether your business is capable of continuous improvement or growth in a dynamic environment. Ideally, you will want both. Through a dynamic environment, you will be subject to change daily. This is due to the legislation and regulations, economic changes or the increased competition. Through this perspective, we are faced with the question, "How can we sustain our ability to achieve our chosen strategy?"

Learning and Growth "To achieve our vision, how will we sustain our ability to change and improve?"	Objectives	Measures	Targets	Initiatives

Simply by looking at the name, you can tell what the balanced scorecard is used for. It will bring balance as it is an essential principle of the scorecard. You bust bring balance between the short-term and long-term objectives, financial and non-financial criteria, leading and lagging indicators as well as the external and internal perspectives. It is about cohesion, which will improve your perspective and must not be an obstacle in another perspective. This cohesion is made more visible as you see it through the connecting lines of the balanced scorecard.

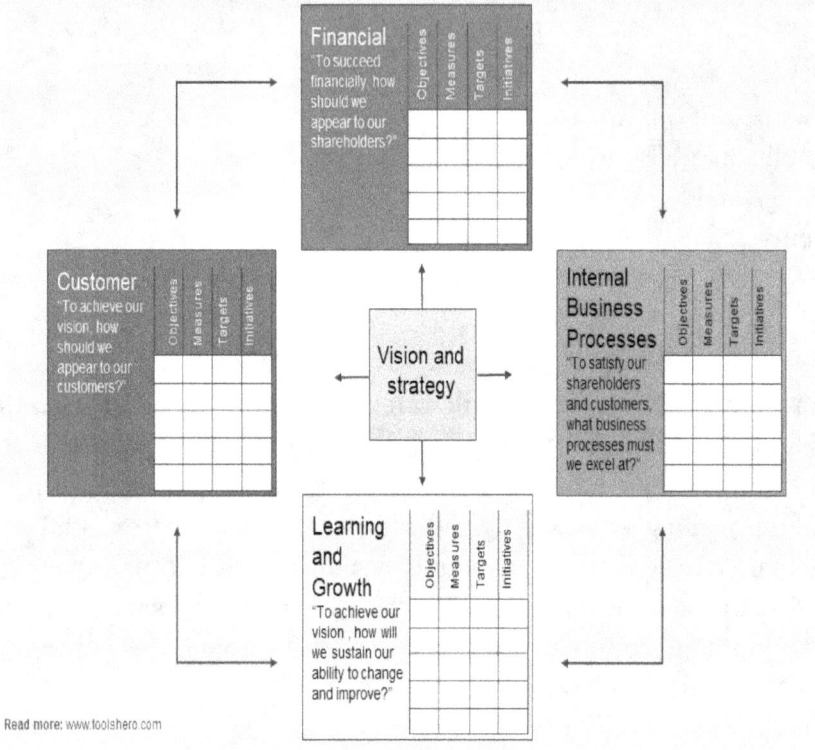

For you to implement the balanced scorecard, several steps will need to be followed. It will start with your senior management setting up a mission, vision and strategy. The strategy will be linked to several objectives that will be referred to as your strategic objectives. From there, the middle management will be informed about the mission, vision and strategic objectives. Through an open discussion, your management can express their opinions which will indicate the critical success factors per the perspectives. They may also point out or set up the indicators themselves for these to be monitored in the future.

Don't forget your financial and customer perspectives. It will be possible to carry out a survey or conduct interviews with the potential shareholders and customers. This will assess what their expectations are. New insight could be provided into the direction of the objectives the necessary objectives. As middle management and senior management consult, there will be several objectives that are formulated in which the different critical success factors are indicated for each objective. These indicators will be used to measure these factors, specify values such as the targets and initiatives that are meant to be achieve through these objectives.

You can also take it one step further by linking your personal objectives to the objectives of your middle management. This will result in that all your personal initiatives will be contributed to the chosen strategy of your business.

There is not one set way to implementing the balanced scorecard. It can be done in different ways or manners. Here are a few simple steps that can get you started.

1. Set up a vision, mission and strategic objectives.
2. Perform a stakeholder analysis to gauge the expectations of your customers and shareholders.
3. Make an inventory of the critical success factors.
4. Translate your strategic objectives into your personal goals.
5. Set up key performance indicators to measure your objectives.
6. Determine the value for your objectives that are to be achieved.
7. Translate your objectives into the operational activities.

Keep in mind; this is not a one-time thing. The process is continuous as a plan-do-check-act and repeat.

Chapter 9 – Fraud and Internal Controls

In today's world, fraud is huge. When you have a business, regardless of the size, there needs to be some protection and internal controls. These controls are your plans that will be implemented for you to safeguard your business assets, ensure its integrity of the accounting records and detect fraud or theft.

There is a big problem with an organization with employee fraud. It does not matter what type, size, location and industry you are in. As an employer, you would like to believe your employees are loyal and working for the benefit of your business. The truth is, most of them probably are. However, there are many reasons why your employees may commit fraud and there are several ways they could do it.

Every business should have a plan for this prevention. With a plan it will be much easier to detect when fraud is present. One type of protection will be through the segregation of duties. This is a highly valuable component of internal control.

Before we can create a plan, start by identifying the types of fraud that could occur. Fraud will mainly be divided into three categories.

Asset Misappropriation: These can be very costly and usually makes up about 90% of all fraud cases. These are the schemes where which your employee steals or exploits your business resources.

Financial Statement Fraud: This type of fraud comprises less than 5% of fraud cases but does cause the most median loss. These are the schemes that involve omitting or intentionally mistaking information in your company's financial reports. It can be a form of fictitious revenues, hidden liabilities or inflated assets. As only specific individuals such as an accountant, bookkeeper or management has access to this information, you have a small pool of individuals that are involved.

Corruption: This type of fraud falls in the middle and is made up of less than 1/3 of fraud cases. These schemes happen when your employees use their influence in a business transaction for the benefits of themselves while violating the duties to their employer. For example, you will see bribery, extortion and conflict of interest.

Fraud Prevention

Prevention of fraud is the one thing that every employer is concerned about. In fact, it is vital to all organizations and businesses. Some of you may not know where to start. Perhaps I can point you in the right direction throughout this chapter. Part of success is the prevention of fraud.

Know Your Employees: When your employee is about to commit some type of fraud, they will show specific behavioral traits that will indicate their intentions. One thing that can help is observing and listening to your employees. It is important for management to get involved with those who work for them. If you are a small business with only a handful of employees, this is easy to detect as you will be more hands-on with everyone who works for you, although not all businesses are small. For those who have several employees among multiple departments, then you must train your supervisors and department managers to look for the same among those who are working with them. A slight change in attitude could give you a clue. This may allow for potential issues to be addressed before fraud is committed. What is sad is often that fraud could be committed by the one employee you did not expect. It is imperative to know your employees and engage them in a conversation. Get to know your employees on a personal level. This will give you an idea of the risks that could be involved if their situations change.

Make Employees Aware and Set Up a Reporting System: Awareness will affect all your employees. From the top management to the clerk at the bottom, everyone should be aware of the fraud risk policy, which includes the types of fraud and the consequences associated with them. Those who are planning to commit fraud will know and understand that the management and fellow co-workers are watching. This will hopefully deter them from wanting to commit fraud against your business. This will give your honest employees the knowledge of the possible signs of fraud or theft and they will not be tempted to commit such an act. You have now empowered your employees to help fight against fraud. It is hard for management to catch everything; however, now you have an entire workforce that watches collectively you can catch a lot more.

Implement Internal Controls: As was stated at the beginning of this chapter; these controls are your plans or programs that will be implemented to safeguard your company's assets, ensure its integrity of the accounting records and detect fraud and theft. *Segregation of duties* will be an essential component of your internal controls and can reduce the risk of fraud within your business. Your *documentation* will be another internal control that can help reduce fraud. Your internal control program should be monitored and revised on a consistent basis. This will ensure they are current and effective with advances in technology. If you do not have this control in place, your business is vulnerable to fraud. I highly suggest you start implementing this program right away.

Monitor Vacation Balances: As an employer, you may be highly impressed by an employee who has not missed a day at work in many years. Even though this sounds like a loyal employee, ask yourself, "Why are they not taking any days off?" Sometimes they just enjoy their job. Ok, most of us do not enjoy work so much that you never take any time off. This is where it is essential to know your employees. This could be a sign that they are hiding something and are worried about getting caught if they take time off from work. This could raise a red flag to watch this employee closer and see if you can detect anything out of the ordinary. Another good idea is to cross train and rotate employees to various jobs within the company. You will not only gain a valuable employee that is well diverse in different areas, but it will help prevent fraud. However, if you suspect fraud, this could also help you to reveal fraudulent activities.

Hire Experts: This may seem like a lot of work to get a good plan in place. Maybe you do not know how to do it. A Certified Fraud Examiner (CFE, Certified Public Accountant (CPA) and CPAs who are Certified in Financial Forensics (CFF) can help you with establishing your antifraud policies and procedures.

Live the Corporate Culture: A positive work environment can help to prevent your employees from committing fraud and theft. Be sure to have a clear organizational structure with written policies and procedures for a fair employment practice. Having an open-door policy is another great fraud prevention system. This will give your employees an open line of communication with the management. As a leader, the business owners and senior management should lead from the front and set the example.

Fraud Detection

Having great prevention strategies are nice; however, you should also have some detection methods in place. At the same time, ensure these methods are visible to your employees. Through the visibility of these controls, it may deter fraudulent behavior. It is important to monitor and update your detection strategies continuously. This will ensure their effectiveness. Your detection plan will usually happen during the regular business day. As you create your detection plan, you will take the external information and link that with your internal data, therefore giving you the results of having a plan that should enhance your prevention controls. Remember, with anything you do within your business, "Communication is the Key to Success." This is also true for your detection plan. Communicating this to all your employees will help your company grow with fewer fraud cases involved.

As we have been considering the issue of fraud and safeguarding your business, I compiled a small list of items that could be implemented in your fight against fraud.

- Implementation of a fraud hotline or web-based portal
- Separation of duties
- Reconciliation of bank accounts and management review
- Review and authorization of expense reimbursements
- Safeguarding and reconciliation of petty cash
- Restrict the use of the company credit card and verify all charges made
- Provide the Board of Directors oversight of the company operations and management
- Prepare all fiscal policies and procedures in writing and obtain approval from the Board of Directors
- Use purchase orders
- Control cash receipts
- Use informal audits
- Install computer security measures
- Track your business checks
- Manage inventory and use a security system
- Beware of the accounts receivable

- Provide a way for your employees to report theft or fraud by a co-worker

These are only a few ways of preventing and detecting fraud. As the owner of your company, take the time to meet with your Board of Directors and senior management. Work together to ensure you have a plan in place, and it is used within your company. There are so many other ways that can help in this fight with fraud. Use what you have and get started now with the internal controls.

Conclusion

You have been a brave accounting ninja in training. There has been so much that we have covered in the past few pages. It has not been a smooth journey, but it has been a rewarding one. The information you have learned is just the beginning. These are the basic tools to help you through your training. Consider this as the foundation. When you start the construction of a new building, you first start with the cornerstone and then build from there.

You have learned many great things in the way of the force. Remember the basic principles in chapter one as they are important for your business to grow and expand. Along with that, many of you may start to trade and do business on an international level. That is the main reason why I felt it was essential to know and understand the policies and principles on a global level.

Granted, all information included in this book is important to achieve great success; however, I want you to focus on a few key areas. I want you to familiarize yourself with the balanced scorecard and the fraud prevention. These two areas will help you safeguard your business and drive it beyond the next level of growth.

This book is not meant to tell you that it is this way and no other way. In fact, you have seen me state many times that it is always changing. In bookkeeping and accounting, the policies are ever updating. I have given you the basic resource for success.

If you want to see your business grow and succeed, then this will help you achieve that goal or at least point in into that direction. One more area of interest will be chapter seven as we talk about budgets. This is a huge aspect of success.

One thing to always remember, "Communication is one of the Keys to a Successful Business."

Preview of Bookkeeping
The Ultimate Guide to Bookkeeping for Small Business

Introduction

Whether you are just starting your business or have had your business for years, it is important to know bookkeeping.

Bookkeeping has been around for centuries. However, it has evolved over time to better help your business keep track of your finances.

Bookkeeping covers a long list of aspects that help the business owner make decisions about the company. To better understand bookkeeping, my goal is to help you get a good feel for knowing how to read the financial reports, the basics of bookkeeping, employees, understanding the balance sheet and income statement, and so much more.

Come along with me as we explore the world of bookkeeping and help you, the business owner, understand how to make sense out of bookkeeping.

As an added bonus, I have included a section for your business taxes. I also included a step-by-step process of preparing W-2 forms and the information that is needed for those. You will soon find out that there is more to it than just providing the information and typing it up on the W-2 form.

Keep reading and you will see what it takes to get on the same page as your bookkeeper. I always said, "It is not the business owner that runs the business. It is the business owner teamed up with the bookkeeper that truly runs the business."

Running a business can be fun and rewarding. However, if you do not have the basic knowledge of the fundamental financial skills needed, it can prove to be stressful as well.

Throughout this book you will learn the basics of bookkeeping and finding the right bookkeeper for you. As you go through it, you will also learn about the ledgers and journals. It is important that you know where your money is at all times. I also take the time to talk to you about hiring employees. Let's face it, if your business is going to grow above a certain level, you will eventually need to hire someone to work with you.

There is also a lot of software available to help you with all your bookkeeping needs, although not all accounting software is right for your business. We will take a look at a few of the top rated applications and give you both the good and bad of each one.

Don't forget, you also need to understand those scary financial statements. That's why we will take a look at the four main financial statements and break them down for you so that you can easily read and understand each one.

It does not matter if you have been in business for a couple of years or are just starting, you will be filing taxes at the end of the year. This is a lot of work and your bookkeeper can help you get prepared. Within the bonus chapter, I included a checklist for small businesses to help you along the way in knowing which documents you need to find and hold on to.

Did you know that as a business owner you can deduct a lot of your expenses? I included that as well. It is only a small list, and with a little research you could probably find more.

Finally, I also included, in detail, how to go about preparing, distributing, and filing the employees' W-2's.

So come along with me as we take this glorious adventure into bookkeeping for small businesses and give you the power to understand your businesses financial health.

Chapter 1 – Bookkeeping Basics

Before we get started on breaking down bookkeeping, we need to look at some of the basics. I want you to have the ability to read your financial records and understand them. This will allow for you to know the financial aspect of your business. In turn, it will allow you to make good decisions that can increase the growth of your business.

Double-Entry Method

Bookkeeping uses a method called the "Double-Entry Bookkeeping." This means that for every entry there is at least one debit and one credit.

I want you to remember this equation:

- Assets = Liabilities + Equity

This is the basic formula for the Double-Entry Method and will come into play with every transaction you make.

Source Documents

Every transaction made will have a source document. Source documents could be anything from a contract to a gas receipt. If you spent the business's money then you will need some form of proof of how much you spent. These are the source documents.

These documents will give us all the information you will need to record it in the books. This includes referencing the source documents. Some software will allow you to attach the scanned file to the transaction so that at any time you can bring up the source document.

End-Of-Period Procedures

End-of-Period Procedures relate to not only quarters. Even though all the transactions have been recorded throughout the months or year, they still are not read for preparing the financial reports.

To ensure that you have your books accurate for preparing the financial reports, you need to consider that there are procedures that need to happen at least at month-end, year-end, and the end of payroll year.

The following outline will show, as a guideline, what should be done during each time.

1. Month-End Procedures
   - Run the Company/Business Data Auditor
   - Reconcile your Bank Accounts
   - Review Reports
   - Send Customer Statements
   - Record Depreciation
   - Pay Payroll Taxes
   - Lock Periods
2. Year-End Procedures (to prepare for the new fiscal year)
   - Complete Month-End Tasks
   - Perform an Inventory Count

- Provide Information to your Accountant
- Enter End-of-Year Adjustments
- Back Up your Company/Business File
- Start New Fiscal Year
- Optimize and Verify your Company/Business File

3. End of Payroll Year (to prepare for new fiscal year) - *NOTE: Do Not Update Tax Tables*
    - Run Your Last Payroll
    - Optimize and Verify your Company/Business File
    - Back Up your Company/Business File
    - Start a New Payroll Year
    - Install Product Updates
    - Run Your First Payroll
    - Restore Your Backup
    - Print Year-End Payroll Forms
    - Print Vendor 1099 Statements
    - Print Payroll Reports

Compile the Adjusted Trial Balance

Making these adjustments are very important. When looking at which adjustments need to be made first, you need to gather and compile a spreadsheet that will allow for your trial balance entries as well as the adjustments.

Keep in mind that these adjustments are for correcting errors in the initial trial balance so that everything will come to balance. This form for the adjustments is an internal form but will be used for helping compile the financial statements. Now that automated systems like Xero and QuickBooks are used, the trial balance worksheet is not often practiced. However, it is still a good source document. This is in part due to the automated systems creating the reports for you.

Here is an example of what the worksheet may look like:

Frank's Financials

Trial Balance

August 31, 20XX

	Unadjusted Trial Balance	Adjusted Entries	Adjusted Trial Balance
Cash	$60,000		$60,000
Accounts Receivable	$180,000	$50,000	$230,000
Inventory	$300,000		$300,000
Fixed Assets (net)	$210,000		$210,000
Accounts Payable	($90,000)		($90,000)
Accrued Liabilities	($50,000)	($25,000)	($75,000)
Notes Payable	($420,000)		($420,000)
Equity	($350,000)		($350,000)
Revenue	($400,000)	($50,000)	($450,000)
Cost of Goods Sold	$290,000		$290,000
Salaries	$200,000	$25,000	$225,000
Payroll Taxes	$20,000		$20,000

Rent	$35,000		$35,000
Other Expenses	$15,000		$15,000
Totals	$0.00	$0.00	$0.00

Closing the Books

When closing your books at the end of a fiscal year, there are 4 areas that will need to be closed. These areas are temporary accounts and should be zeroed out at the end of each fiscal year.

First, create an Income Summary account. This is considered a holding area.

Closing the Revenue Accounts

The first area that needs to be addressed are the revenue accounts. You will either Debit or Credit this account to close it out and have a zero balance. Then you will either Debit or Credit the Income Summary account to add that balance to the account. Remember if you Debit or Credit one account you must do the opposite for the other account to keep the books balanced.

Closing the Expense Accounts

The second set of accounts are the expense accounts. You will do the same with these accounts as you did with the Revenue accounts. You must close out all expense accounts.

Balancing the Income Summary

By name you should have an increase in the income summary for the revenue and a decrease for each of the expenses. Keep in mind that if the expenses are more than the revenue then it will be a negative number and considered a loss. However, if the revenue is more than the expenses then it is a gain or profit for that year.

Closing the Income Summary

The last step in closing the book is to Debit or Credit the income summary account and do the same to the Retained Earnings Account, leaving a zero balance in the income summary account.

Preparing Reports

A pretty important step is to prepare the reports or financial statements. Although there are so many reports that can be created, we are going to focus on the main reports as they are what is needed for a small business.

As a bookkeeper, you will need to get very familiar with the following reports:

- The Balance Sheet
- Income Statement
- Statement of Retained Earnings
- Statement of Cash Flow

Later in this book we will look more closely at each one of these statements and how to read them so that you can make sense out of your businesses financial standings.

Check out this book!

Preview of Accounting

The Ultimate Guide to Accounting for Beginners – Learn the Basic Accounting Principles

Introduction

This book is intended for people who want to know something about the fundamentals of financial accounting without becoming an accountant. Many people are in this position; small business owners, employers, employees, business owners, stockholders, investors, and many, many more. Most of these folks do not need a deep understanding of accounting, they just need to learn what accounting is and how they should be using it. Just as important, they need to understand what accountants are talking about in their reports. They must learn the vocabulary and the most important terms. The product of accounting is information, important information for that wide range of stakeholders.

We will examine this subject in some detail, discussing accounting fundamentals, the various areas where accounting professionals work and the information they produce. We will also examine the measures and ratios that accountants use to analyze an organization's performance and the important relationship between time and money. The fact that information is the product of accounting will remain foremost in this book.

Chapter 1 - Accounting is Different From Bookkeeping

Accounting is not bookkeeping. Bookkeeping concentrates on recording the organization's financial activities, whatever the business in which they are engaged. Maybe that is retail sales, home construction or manufacturing. No matter what business activity is taking place, someone must keep track of the transactions; selling, buying, repairing equipment, everything of significance. And in fact, even individuals must learn about accounting and must do certain bookkeeping tasks for their own personal finances, like balancing their checkbook and establishing personal budgets.

If the business is engaged in retail sales, bookkeepers record every sale, every purchase of inventory and every employee's pay. That is bookkeeping.

Accountants take this information and analyze, summarize and report the results. Remember, the product of accounting is information. This information is vital to management for their operating and investment decisions. Management must know how much money the business has, how much inventory it holds, how many employees are retained and how much they are being paid.

The viewpoint of a bookkeeper is the details. The viewpoint of an accountant is much broader and at a higher level. The accountant must be able to advise management on many decisions; how many more employees can be hired, what taxes are due and how to minimize them, analyzing investment decisions, and so forth.

Let's look at an example. Riverside Machine Company is a small manufacturer of components for the automobile industry. Their clients include almost all of the automobile manufacturers, and they are very busy when the industry is thriving.

The owners of Riverside are concerned about reducing manufacturing costs for a certain type of part that requires a lot of machining on several different types of machines. The engineers have determined that they can increase the rate of production by installing robots to load and unload the machines and transfer parts between them. The company has several robotic systems in operation now and is confident of their ability to incorporate these new robots. Currently, there is a serious backlog of work for these machines and improving the workflow would allow faster delivery with less overtime and not needing to work weekends to maintain production.

The engineers have determined all the necessary information related to this investment in terms of robot costs, tools needed by the robots, increases in production rate and effect on delivery time. They then sit down with the accounting experts to compute the improvements in cost, reductions in labor costs, shortening of delivery time and so forth. The accountant then uses all of this information to compute the effects on the firm's financial performance and profitability.

In most companies, the accountants compute a value for "Internal Rate of Return" for decisions by management. This rate of return serves as a threshold for new projects. It becomes one of the considerations used by management to decide whether or not to make the investment, in this case, in the new robots. Other considerations of course include delivery improvements, customer satisfaction, product quality and several others. That is a proper role for the accountant working with the engineers.

In addition to being a source of reliable financial information on these kinds of decisions, the accounting department also acts as what can be described as a "Scorekeeper", by monitoring costs and revenues, leading to profitability for the firm. This information is reported to management on a regular basis to help guide ongoing management decisions. The accountants cannot do much at all to influence the profitability of the firm directly, but their role is to report findings to management for them to make decisions.

The accounting function also leads the efforts at budgeting and budget reporting. These are more examples of the accounting product of information. These reports are available in varying levels of detail for publically owned companies and non-profit organizations. Privately owned companies are not required to publish these reports, except for those required by the government, regulatory and taxing authorities.

In their role as providers of information, they are often called upon for informed recommendations to help management decision making.

Chapter 2 - Understanding the Vocabulary

Every special area of interest has its own vocabulary, and accounting is the same. Many of the words used will be familiar to the reader but may have certain shades of meaning that are important. We need to understand this vocabulary. Here are some key definitions that are important to the accounting function.

Asset: an asset is anything the organization owns that helps it accomplish its mission. For a fast food restaurant, the grill or stove in the kitchen area is an asset. For a retail store, the inventory in the back room is an asset, along with display cases and shelves.

Liability: a liability is anything the organization owes to someone else. Unpaid wages to employees is a liability, taxes owed to the local government is a liability, unpaid insurance premiums for employee healthcare policies is a liability, bills for inventory that have not been paid is a liability.

Equity: equity is a measure of the claim of someone on the assets of the organization, such as liabilities (claims by the person or entity to whom the liability is owed, such as loans from a bank) and the investment by the owners of the organization.

Income: money flowing into the organization from its operations in whatever the line of business might be, for example, sales in a fast food restaurant, or rent collected on property the business owns.

Expense: this is the amount of money the organization needs to spend in order to carry out its operations. This represents payments to asset and service providers. For example, payments to a supplier of inventory items for a retail store.

Distributions: outflows of money to owners or stockholders, or bonuses to employees at the end of the year, for example.

Cash Flow: the term cash flow represents the money flowing through the operation, essentially income minus expenses. You can imagine a stream of money flowing into the organization with small streams going out as distributaries to pay for liabilities. The flow that is moving through this stream is the cash flow. How much is left at the end of the process is the profit for the firm.

Overhead: this is a group of costs not directly associated with the major function of the organization but necessary in order to make the organization accomplish its goals. For example, in a hospital, the janitorial staff that cleans and sanitizes the buildings, rooms and equipment are not directly associated with the hospital's patients, but they are absolutely essential. The labor and other costs like cleaning and sanitizing supplies are part of the organization's overhead. All the other myriad of costs like electricity, lighting, lawn maintenance, and even sweeping the parking lot are essential but not directly tied to the patients and their care. The accounting office is considered overhead for any organization not involved in the Public Accounting business.

GAAP: This is the term used to describe the Generally Accepted Accounting Principles. This is a set of 'rules' for the accounting profession, which must be followed to assure an accurate description of the financial activities of the organization. GAAP applies to all organizations that function in commerce, public service, and all other sectors of the general economy. Following these GAAP rules assures the public, the stockholders, the donors to non-profit organizations, the owners, employees and the taxing and regulatory authorities that the accounting for the organization is done in accordance with the proper methods and systems.

Each country establishes its own accounting standards but there exists an International Accounting Standards Board responsible for establishing and accrediting accounting standards for all nations who subscribe. Similarly, many countries establish similar Boards, to promulgate and enforce standards through certification and audit systems. These are in the form of standards, conventions and rules. Companies are not necessarily required to follow them but any publicly traded company must conform to the established Accounting Practices.

Chapter 3 – Accounting Reports: The Income Statement

Remember that the product of accounting is information. The three most common forms for that information are the "Income Statement", the "Balance Sheet", and the "Cash Flow Statement." Every organization uses some form of these three documents and usually all three. We will explore the Balance Sheet in Chapter 4 and the Cash Flow Statement in Chapter 5.

The Income Statement or Profit and Loss Statement (or P&L statement) can be imagined as a video tape of the organization over some period of time, like a month, six months or a year. This statement tells management how the firm is doing from the standpoint of "Are we making money or not?" Of course, this is a very fundamental question, since after a number of periods of losses, the firm will no longer be viable and will go out of business.

The most important use of the Income Statement is to compare it with prior periods and with the period budget. If management has determined that the firm must meet certain performance levels, they need the answer to the question above; "How are we doing compared with our goals and budget?" Each organization has an established and agreed upon budget. The budget contains allocations of resources for all of the activities of the organization, from sales, purchases of materials for sale or production, employee salaries and benefits and even overhead items like electricity and water.

These budgets are set up, usually each year, to guide the managers and supervisors in what decisions can be made to commit resources like money and labour, and for what purposes. Based on this budget, which has been agreed upon by management, it acts as a steering mechanism for the firm's operations. The periodic P&L reports represent the Accounting function's role in keeping score. Here is an example of a P&L Statement or an Income Statement. We will look at each of these entries to see what they represent, based on The Martin Company.

THE MARTIN COMPANY, INC.
INCOME STATEMENT
(FIRST HALF, 2014)
JANUARY 1, 2014 THROUGH JUNE 30, 2014

(all amounts in thousands of dollars)

Sales, Gross: $116,410

Less: Returns and Allowances: $3,075

Net Sales: $113,335

Less Cost of Goods Sold: $78,683

Less Current Depreciation Charges: $1,450

Gross Profit: $33,202

Operating Expenses

Selling and Promotion: $18,005

General and Administration: $8,910

Total Operating Expenses: $26,915

Operating Profit: $6,287

(Gross Profit minus Operating Expense)

Other Income and Expense

Interest and Dividend Income: $363

less: Interest Expense: $917

Net Interest Expense: $554

Profit Before Taxes: $5,733

Taxes on Income at 35%: $2,007

Net Profit: $3,726

This P&L or Income Statement is for the Martin Company. The Martin Company manufacturers small household appliances, which are sold through distributors under Martin's label and major discount and department stores under their labels. Manufacturing operations are located in a small town in the Midwest. The key technologies employed by the firm include manufacturing of fractional horsepower motors, injection molding of plastic parts and machining of miscellaneous small metal parts such as shafts, armatures and gears as well as assembly of the products, packaging and shipping them to customers.

As it says at the top, this report covers the first half of the year. For this company, their budget year is a calendar year. Some organizations may use other budget years. Government organizations often use October 1 through September 30 as a budget year. A mid-year report is very valuable to management, to keep track of performance, especially in complex organizations.

Total Sales; The first line entered is the total sales for that period. This is the value of products shipped to customers. In some cases, there may be returns from customers for any number of reasons; wrong color, wrong address, quality issues, and so forth. This is recorded as Returns and Allowances and is subtracted from Gross Sales resulting in Net Sales.

Cost of Goods Sold; The line labeled Cost of Goods Sold represents the cost that Martin incurred in producing the products shipped during that period. That will include the materials and components purchased, the labor used to produce these products and may include machine time if that is the procedure for Martin Company.

Depreciation; Martin Company must also account for the wear and tear on their productive assets ranging from big, expensive plastic injection molding machines to company vehicles. This is a real cost that must be accounted for but is not a cash expense. It is determined by the accounting office and along with the Cost of Goods Sold, reduces the net sales to give the amount of Gross Profit. This loss of value of assets is called depreciation and is subtracted from sales, even though it is not a cash expense. Depreciation will be covered in a later section.

Operating Expenses; However, this is not the complete picture of costs incurred. The items labeled Operating Expenses include the salaries of the supervisors, managers, sales representatives, shipping operators, energy costs like electric power and gas, office expenses for papers, copiers, and the myriad of other costs necessary to produce the products that generate sales income. In some companies, this lump of costs may be referred to as "Overhead." Overhead is a necessary expense and must be included in the budget and in P&L statement. Managers and supervisors work hard to keep Overhead costs to a minimum. Overhead also includes taxes paid on the real estate and other ad valorum taxes. These amounts are shown as Selling and Promotion as well as General and Administrative or G&A. G&A usually includes the Overhead costs.

Operating Profit; After accounting for the Operating Expenses, we are left with the Operating Profit. Operating Profit is the first measure of how effective Martin Company is in carrying out its main objective, making and selling products. Operating Profit is the Gross Profit minus the Operating Expenses.

Other Income and Expense; But, Martin Company must also take into account the other costs such as interest on loans they need to purchase equipment and materials. They may have other incidental income from sources like investments, rental property receipts and royalties. These are all included in the P&L statement but are not part of the major business, making and selling products.

Profit Before Taxes; When all of that is included, we see the Profit Before Taxes or PBT. That profit must be reduced by the taxes paid on the sales and other income, and we finally get to see the profits resulting from the major business of Martin. This is what managers call the "Bottom Line."

Managers and supervisors are vitally concerned with how the P&L Statement compares with the budget and how it is changing over time. Are we earning more profit this year than we did in the same period last year and in prior years? Continual growth in profit makes it possible of Martin to stay in business, producing products, serving customers and employing people. It is also essential to being able to expand the business, adding more products and investing in advanced technologies that customers demand.

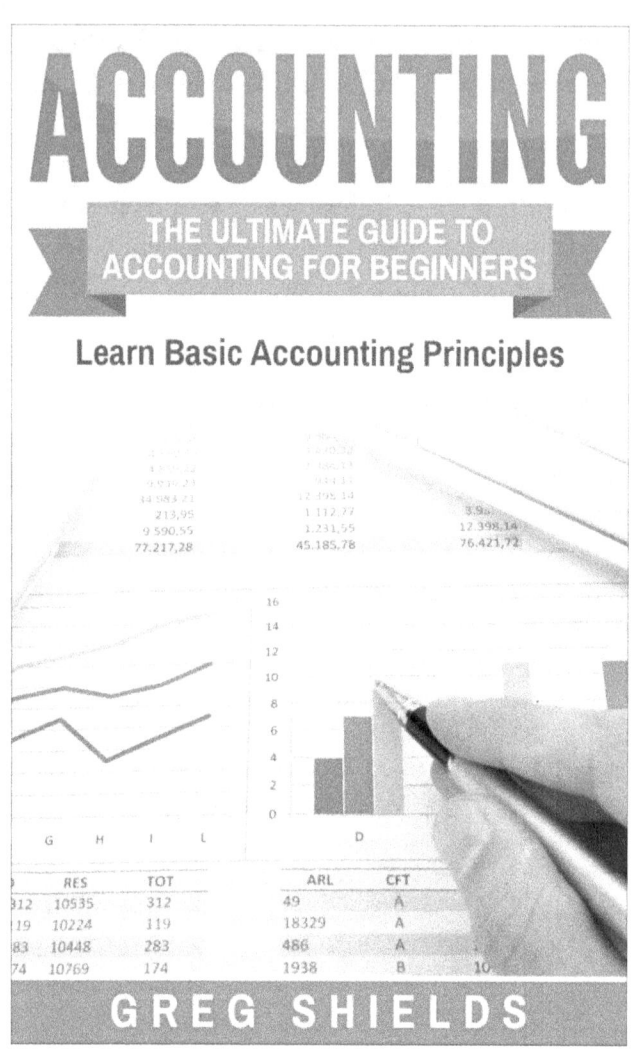

Check out this book!

www.ingramcontent.com/pod-product-compliance
Lightning Source LLC
Chambersburg PA
CBHW052329220526
45472CB00001B/344